ANGER MANAGEMENT FOR PARENTS

EFFECTIVE STRATEGIES TO MASTER YOUR EMOTIONS, UNDERSTAND TRIGGERS, IMPROVE COMMUNICATION, AND RAISE CONFIDENT CHILDREN IN A PEACEFUL HOME

T. NICOLE

NONFICTION
NUCLEUS

TABLE OF CONTENTS

INTRODUCTION

You've just made it to the line for check out at a crowded grocery store. There's someone ahead of you, and you are beginning to get nervous. Your toddler has spent the entirety of the trip grabbing every snack they pass and trying to throw it in your cart. You've wrestled more bags of chips out of their small hands than you can count. You know you are running out of time, and your child is running out of patience, when you hear them tell you for the fourth time that they have to use the potty. You don't bother to remind them that you asked them to use it before you left the house. You start loading your groceries onto the belt, and your anxiety kicks up when you realize that your child has decided to help themselves to a bag of M&M's. You snatch it out of their hands with more force than you would like and dodge the judgmental looks of the people behind you while you gather the money from your purse to pay.

You are finally ready to leave, and you listen to the grating of the shopping cart wheels all the way to your car. You settle your humming child into their car seat, load the groceries into the trunk, and head home. You are almost home when your child loudly announces from the back seat that they've had an accident, and before you can even think, you explode.

You tell them that they've behaved badly the entire time you were in the store. You yell that they touched everything they could, and that they were noisy and rude. You scream that they embarrassed you, and that they never, ever just listen. That's all you want, for them to listen. They begin to cry as you end your tirade, and now you feel guilty, so you stare out of the windshield in silence for the rest of the drive home.

Does this sound familiar? The hectic shopping trip, the misbehaving child, or the emotional outburst that crept in at the last moment?

Before we go any further, let's get something straight.

The most important thing you can learn from this book is that you are not alone. If this story is your life, even if it's just a different version, you are not a bad parent. There are parents all over the world that are just like you, and they are struggling. Parents who have let the anger get the best of them, parents who just don't know how to change the cycle. Statistics will tell you that a significant number of parents admit to regularly expressing anger towards their children.

Most parents who struggle with this know that anger has found a permanent place in their homes. They know that it makes them do things that they think they shouldn't, and that they feel horrible when the frustration wins. They know that they need to change. They have pieces of the picture, but not enough for it to really make a difference.

If you are here, this book is for you. If you've ever felt the heat of anger rising when you are with your child, this book is for you. It's for every parent who has ever paused, breathless, after a heated exchange with their child. It's for those parents that can't shake the nagging guilt that follows them after they get their feelings out. It's for the parents that have started their journey into managing their anger and are just looking for some techniques to bring them to the finish line. It's for first-time parents who are afraid of continuing a cycle of unhealthy anger and want to know how to stop it before it starts.

One thing that is universal for parents, including me and you, is that we want a safe, healthy environment for our children to grow up in. I was the parent from the story, I was stressed and struggling, and feeling like no matter what I did, things didn't get better. I am here, because this journey is about more than just managing anger, it's about paving the way to a more harmonious life. It's about building stronger, more empathetic relationships with our children. It's about doing the work now, so our children don't have to do it later. I am here because while there is no easy way to do it, you don't have to do it alone.

Together, we are going to do the work. We are going to explore this anger that overwhelms us sometimes. We will learn why it happens, and what some of the most common triggers of anger are. We will walk through why it can be so hard to control our emotions. We will take a good look at what it can do to us and our children if we don't take the time to learn how to change it. Most importantly, we will take a look at what the statistics don't tell us. Exactly how to make the change.

Together, we will take measured steps toward a future where anger no longer has a foothold in our homes. It will make room for more love, understanding, and joy in our families.

1

WHAT IS ANGER?

In the day-to-day of parenting, anger can often cut in, uninvited, and take the lead. It's not the scenario we rehearsed, and it is obviously not something we are proud of. It's certainly not what we imagined when we first held our children. Yet here we are, filled with an anger that we don't understand.

Scenario:

It's a Saturday morning, and you are glad to have some time to relax after the long work week. Unfortunately, you can't sleep in, because your teenager has soccer practice in an hour, but things could be worse.

You are walking downstairs to the kitchen to make a cup of coffee, because for most of us parent's, coffee is survival. You're on the third step when you almost fall because someone decided to leave their paw patrol doll on the stairs.

You bring it to the playroom and can't help but clench your fists when you realize you will be spending a large part of your day cleaning the room, again. In the kitchen, you are rolling your shoulders and stirring your coffee, when you hear the fridge door open behind you. You can hear your child grunting as they grab a gallon of milk, and you turn just in time to see it fall and crash into the tiled floor. Just like that, all of your hopes for a relaxing day seem to vanish.

UNDERSTANDING THE BIOLOGICAL DEFINITIONS OF ANGER

Over the years, our understanding of anger has evolved, thankfully. In the past, it was seen as a character flaw, or even a lapse in morality. Which is probably why we as parents feel so bad when it gets the best of us. Today, we know that the emotion is far more complex than that, which extends a bit of grace to those of us that struggle with it.

Anger is our response to feeling like something is wrong, or that someone has done something to us that is not okay. It is an emotional response that every person in the world has felt at one point or another.

We know that it has happened to everyone, because it is a biological response that we are born with, and it doesn't just affect us mentally. The brain is a marvel of evolution, a command center that controls our thoughts, emotions, and actions with astonishing precision. It communicates to all of the nerves, muscles, and organs in your body to make sure you have everything you need. Your amygdala is a small part of your brain, and it is where your emotions are processed.

When your amygdala thinks that the body is being threatened, which is how it feels when it processes anger, it leaps into action to protect you. Unfortunately for us, our brain is unable to tell the difference between a real and perceived threat. This means that it has an annoying habit of overreacting. When our anger begins to rise in uncomfortable situations, it is because the brain is doing just that, sensing a threat and overreacting. It does not understand that stepping on a toy is not actually a danger, and so it sends a cascade of signals to tell our body to prime itself to react anyway.

The prefrontal cortex typically helps us make educated, responsible decisions. It also helps us balance the repercussions of our actions. Ideally, this rational part of the brain would step in here and help us out. However, when anger surges, the rapid response from the amygdala can easily overshadow the prefrontal cortex. What does this lead to for those of us who just walked into a tornado in the playroom? It leads to impulsive decisions that we will most likely regret later, like slamming doors, and shouting harsh words. When the rational part of our brain is not in the driver seat, we can find ourselves in situations that are not in tune with our intentions, values, and morals.

Our hormones can also influence our emotional state and lead to anger. The impact of our hormones cannot be overstated, especially because we are normally unaware of when they are being released. They can flood our systems with a cocktail of chemicals and leave us wondering why we suddenly felt like it was a good idea to scream at our child for spilling milk. When we encounter a stressor, our adrenal glands release a bunch of hormones, including adrenaline and cortisol. These are the body's mobilizing agents, and they create the "fight or flight" response our ancestors once relied on for survival.

While we might have been thankful for this response in the stone age, now it can cause more trouble than it is worth. The hormones can contribute to instability in moments where we are already teetering on the edge. Adrenaline increases our heart rate and blood pressure, sending more blood to our muscles, sharpening our senses, and intensifying our emotions. While this is helpful in life threatening situations, it can be detrimental to our emotional reactions if we aren't aware of it. Cortisol, often referred to as the stress hormone, regulates many processes in the body, including immune response and metabolism. In the short term, it aids in the fight or flight response, but its long-term presence can lead to a host of health issues.

In the heat of a stressful parenting moment like the one described above; these hormones can flood our system. It's not unlike a surge protector being overwhelmed by a sudden voltage spike, leading to a short circuit. The sudden spike of hormones, rapidly beating heart, and increased blood pressure can easily manifest as an outburst of anger.

We react just as strongly to emotional stressors as we might to a physical one. The heart races, the palms sweat, and muscles tense, all to prepare to confront the challenge head-on. But in a world where our issues are often emotional rather than physical, this physiological response doesn't always serve us well.

In our world, it can leave us thinking that we are a bad parent, that we aren't doing enough, or that we are not in control.

Anger alerts us to perceived threats, injustices, or frustrations, it is a signal. It is critical to understand these emotions are not statements about who we are, but about how we are feeling. Rather than saying "I am angry," which glues our identity to emotion, it's more helpful to say, "I feel angry." This small shift in language reinforces the concept that anger is a momentary experience, it is not a permanent state of being, and it will pass.

Recognizing emotion as a signal also enables us to look more deeply into its causes. Is the anger a reaction to a specific behavior of our child, or indicative of a deeper, unmet need within ourselves? By asking such questions, we can uncover the root of our anger and address it in a positive way. So, while we can't stop our bodies from overreacting in what seems like the worst of times, we can do something. We can look for the signs that we might be beginning to feel stressed or angry. We can give ourselves a head start, so we have time to come up with a game plan before it's too late. Here are some signals that might mean that anger is beginning to creep in:

Physical:

- Increased heart rate

- Sweating

- Rising temperature, feeling hot

- Clenching your jaw or fist

- Tensed muscles

- Dizziness

- Headache

- Stomachache

- Rubbing your head

Emotional:

- The desire to leave the situation.

- Feeling anxious

- Feeling like you want to lash out.

- Feeling sad or depressed

- Increase in irritability.

- A decrease in patience

So, what do you do, when you realize that your body's natural response to stressful situations leaves you and our children feeling unstable? The easy answer is, we don't let our instincts win, and we learn. We learn why it happens, to us and our children, aside from the biological reasons. We learn about ourselves and how we react to anger when it rears its ugly head. We learn about our children, and how we affect them when we are angry. We learn how to identify anger when it is being sneaky, and we learn techniques to manage it in healthy, responsible ways. After we have learned all of this, we go to work putting things into practice. Throughout the book you will find small scenarios, use them as opportunities to see the tools we are going to learn, work in a real-life scenario.

Put it into action:

Think back to the scenario in the beginning of this chapter. Only this time, you are going to start the work, the night *before* the incident. You've worked all week and you are tired. You need a good night's rest, because for you maybe lack of sleep is a trigger. So, you are going to prepare your children's clothes the night before, and maybe even skip the last episode of peaky blinders to get to bed on time.

When you start to roll your shoulders at the kitchen counter the next morning, you are going to recognize it for what it is, a distress signal your body is sending you. So many times, we as parents, rob ourselves of the empathy we need. Yes, the day just began, and maybe you think you shouldn't need a break so soon, but you are going to give it to yourself anyway. You are going to turn around to go to the living room for a time-out. You will start releasing the tension in each of your muscles, one by one, while breathing rhythmically. When you're done, you are going to have a renewed sense of patience and feel relaxed.

Maybe, recognizing the need for a time out even lets you catch your child before they drop the gallon of the milk. Even if it doesn't, you've given yourself a few minutes of clarity and a clean slate to attack the problem with. Recognizing the anger, before it brews over, can be the difference between an opportunity for self-care, and an emotional outburst you will regret later.

2

YOUR ANGER IS NOT YOU

Your anger is not you. When the heat of anger rises, it can feel all-consuming, as though the emotion is a part of our being. It is so important to draw a distinction between ourselves and the anger we experience. This realization—that we are not defined by our emotions—is liberating. It allows us to view anger as a temporary state rather than a fixed aspect of our character. Separating yourself from your emotions is a basic fundamental concept in many therapeutic approaches, including cognitive-behavioral therapy. It involves recognizing that while we may have angry feelings, that is not who we are.

It is however really important that as parents we do understand who we are. We need to know where we came from, what makes us tick, and what makes us explode. Knowing these things about ourselves lets us take a step back and look at things objectively. It gives us a better chance at winning against the anger.

Scenario:

It's a Wednesday night and you are sitting at the table with your children. You are eating steak, mashed potatoes, and broccoli. You are feeling proud because you took the time to make a fresh baked pie for after dinner. One by one your children finish their food, and ask to be excused, except for your picky 6-year-old. He's cleared his plate of mashed potatoes and steak but refuses to eat anything else. You've worked hard on the meal, and the fact that he never eats anything other than carbs and candy makes you feel like a bad parent.

He tries a couple of times to get up from the table, and you set him back down and tell him he isn't leaving until he's finished his food. He screams no, and starts to cry, and you can feel your heart start to race. He tells you that it's yucky, and he isn't going to eat it. You fight with him for a few more minutes before you give up and decide that you aren't going to chase him around again.

An hour passes and it's time for bed, and your 6-year-old does not want to go to sleep. He goes to the bathroom, asks for a drink, and demands his favorite stuffed animal. He does anything he can to avoid going to sleep. Each time you talk to him your voice gets a little bit louder. Finally, he tells you that he is hungry. You bring him to the kitchen, heat up the leftovers from his plate from dinner and set it in front of him. He screams NO, knocks the plate onto the floor, and you see red. So, you grab him up, and send him to bed.

I have some good news for you, you are not angry for no reason. You didn't just wake up in the morning and decide to hate the world. You aren't a bad person, and you aren't a bad mom or dad. We've all been there, judging ourselves, and a large portion of us are still there. We want to be the parent who can sit and play with dolls or read bedtime stories with funny voices. The bad news is, chances are if you are here, you are probably not that parent, right now. Your life probably looks more like rushing through bedtime so that you can breathe or getting a little too worked up over the glass of orange juice that spilled all over the breakfast table. So, you aren't an angry person, or a bad person, or a bad parent, but what are you? What you are, is triggered.

WHAT ARE TRIGGERS?

I'm sure we've all heard the term pet peeve in our lives, and it's a good starting point for understanding triggers. A trigger is something that gets under our skin, in the worst possible way. If this analogy doesn't work for you, you can think about a literal trigger. Someone presses it, and something bad happens. The action in itself seems really simple, the reaction is anything but.

When a trigger is activated, we have an instantaneous and often dramatic reaction to it. It's involuntary, and we don't have a choice in what it does to us physically and mentally. Especially if we are unaware of the trigger in the first place. Different triggers can cause different emotions. When it comes to anger, a common theme for parents is that the trigger will lead to actions we are not happy with.

The danger of triggers lies in the fact that a majority of people don't know about them, understand them, and that they are an involuntary response. For so many of us, life, and parenting, require a sense of control. It can be very easy to feel out of control when you don't understand why you are so angry all of the time. Feeling out of control can then make you feel angrier, and the cycle continues.

It can be scary to feel like you aren't in control of your emotions, and it is easy to feel like you are failing when you lose it with your children over, and over. So, we are going to get ahead of it. We are going to learn what some of the most common triggers are and take a look at the responses they bring out of us. When you are looking at the list below, you will probably see quite a few things that bother you. What you want to do is identify the ones that rob you of your self-control, not just the ones that make you a little bit annoyed.

Examples of common triggers:

- **Lack of sleep:** Someone who is triggered by a lack of sleep might find themselves lashing out after a night of tossing and turning. They might be less able to engage in activities both at work and at home.

- **Feeling ignored:** This is the classic case of calling your child's name ten times, and feeling like they are deliberately trying to make you angry by not responding to you.

- **Pain:** This could look like someone being thrown into a rage because they stepped on a toy, banged their elbow on a dresser drawer, or because their child kicked them while they were playing.

- **Being told no**: A parent being triggered by being told no might look like raising their voice when their child says that they won't clean up their room or eat the last piece of broccoli left on their plate.

- **Interruptions**: Having a child interrupt during a conversation or an important work email might leave a triggered parent using harsh words or lashing out.

- **Waiting:** Think back to the story in the beginning of the book. The parent waiting in a grocery line, or maybe in a car in traffic might feel triggered to lash out.

- **Invasions of privacy:** Some people cannot stand to have their personal items touched or moved. This could be the parent that brings work home and explodes when pudding ends up on an important document.

- **Clutter/Mess:** This is the parent that is irritable, yelling, or maybe even raging silently when they find their children's room a mess.

- **Being late:** Some parents' moods are severely affected when they are running late. Their emotions are running high, and they might have an emotional outburst to relieve some of the pressure they are feeling.

- **Public image:** This is the parent who feels anxious and judged when their child is dirty, or when they are throwing a fit in the middle of the grocery store. They feel embarrassed and might take it out on their child.

Being triggered can leave you unable to react reasonably in situations where you might otherwise be able to. Outbursts after being triggered can then leave us feeling out of control, guilty, and sad.

What are my personal triggers?

Most of the triggers above would bother any parent to a certain degree. The vital part of understanding triggers is knowing which ones take you out of the driver's seat. Another danger of triggers is the behaviors that they encourage. It wouldn't be a big deal that you didn't get a good night's sleep, if you were able to wake up the next morning and get through the day peacefully. Your triggers are the ones that severely affect your mental health, the ones that make you treat your children in a way that goes against your values and morals.

While there are millions of other parents who share issues with anger management, each will have their own personal triggers. These triggers can be used as an early warning system to avoid emotional outbursts. Understanding what specifically ignites your anger is a critical step toward better managing your behavior. Recognizing what sets you off, gives you the ability to organize your day-to-day activities in a way that can help you avoid triggers, and in turn, outbursts.

Chances are while you were reading, one or two of these triggers probably hit home for you. What we want to do is find and acknowledge those behaviors or interactions that hit our not-so-sweet spot. To identify your triggers, reflect on moments of anger and look for patterns. Are there certain times of day you're more susceptible? Do particular behaviors from your children consistently provoke a strong reaction?

Documenting these triggers can be enlightening. You will likely learn something about yourself that you didn't know before. Note the events that lead you to feel emotionally overwhelmed, or to react in anger. Over time, this log will reveal your personal triggers, allowing you to anticipate and prepare for them.

GENERATIONAL CYCLES

The reason why family systems are so important is because they mold children. From the day we were born, we have been taught how to interact with the world, by the people that are closest to us. Think of the term, like mother like daughter. Sociology would call the people closest to us in our early years our primary social groups. First it is your parents and siblings, and then it is our teachers and peers, and eventually our friends and coworkers. The lessons you learn in the early years of life follow you forever, because they are supposed to, right?

For the lucky ones, this can be a really good thing. Some people are taught from an early age to listen, understand, and manage their emotions. They are given tools to use when the world seems overwhelming. They are equipped to walk out of their homes and deal with the world without feeling uneasy or over pressured.

For others, the generational cycles and behaviors taught to us as children can be detrimental. They can color the way we see the world and dictate how we interact with our children. They can contribute to us acting out in anger, without us ever suspecting that it might be happening.

If you are going to do the work to become a calmer, happier parent, you need to unpack the unconscious emotional baggage you have from when you were a child. You cannot change something you don't understand. It might surprise you to see how many of the ways you act with your children, and the rules you set for them, are directly tied to your own childhood. There are some people who walk through life and don't bother to pause and understand why they are the way they are, don't be one of them.

What are generational cycles?

You might have heard the term generational curse before. For the purpose of this book, we are just going to call them cycles. Not all of the dynamics you learned in childhood are negative, and even those that are, can teach us some really valuable lessons.

Picture this:

You are eight years old, and you are sitting at the dinner table. You have a napkin neatly folded on your lap. You are eating your food when you hear your father tell your mother something about one of the neighbors, Mrs. May. You ask your father what he said, because you want to feel included in the conversation, and because you are friends with Mrs. May's son. This makes your father angry, and he tells you that children should be seen and not heard. He raises his voice and asks you how many times he has to tell you that adult conversations should not be interrupted. He sends you to your room without supper and slams your door after setting you in bed.

Being interrupted might have been a trigger for your father. Years later, hearing your child try to engage in conversation with adults might be a trigger for you. After all, you were taught that it is not okay. Your child doing this, might bring up old feelings from when you were a child, making you dislike it even more. It might dredge up the loneliness you felt in your room by yourself, or the racing heart beat the slamming of the door caused. What is really important here, is asking yourself if the behavior is really wrong, if it is really harmful? Is it really disrespectful for your child to want to talk with you and your spouse, or with you and a friend? They likely are just looking to be included, and to spend time with you. Your childhood makes you feel like that's bad, but is it really?

Now, this is a mild version of a generational cycle, and it is only one of many. You might need the house to be squeaky clean all the time, because you were yelled at as a child if it wasn't. You might micromanage your child's diet, because you couldn't leave the table with an empty plate. You might even believe that physically punishing a child can be justified, because it was done to you.

What we need to do as parents is recognize what values are important to us for our children to portray. What "rules" do you want them to live by? Know why you are asking your child to do this or that. Know why it is important if they don't listen to you. Know that the way you are parenting your child has been thought out and is not just the remnant of an age-old technique that has been proven not to work, or maybe just doesn't work for you.

How do they affect me?

Generational cycles, just like triggers, can affect you in a host of different ways. They are deeply ingrained actions that you don't really even think about anymore. Here are just a few small samples of the ways generational cycles can affect you.

- **Self-image:** When we are little, we listen to what our parents and siblings say about us, and we believe them. It sounds so simple, but the effects their words can have on us are almost unimaginable. Imagine your parents telling you constantly how hard they have to work to support you. How they have to put food on the table, and clothes on your back, and how they never have a moment's rest. This probably makes you feel like a burden, and if you don't do the work to heal, this will become a part of you. You may look at yourself as a burden and isolate yourself from meaningful relationships. You may decide that you'd rather suffer in silence than have to ask someone for help because it might stress them out.

- **Relationships**: Take for instance the girl who watched her mother and father throw verbal insults at each other every time they had a disagreement. She may grow up to believe that this is what a marriage looks like. She might foster relationships with partners that are centered around conflict, because to her, this is what home feels like. Alternatively, she might have trouble forming long lasting relationships because she is verbally abusive and can't see the problem with it. The most important teachers in her life showed her that is the way relationships work after all.

- **Parenting**: Imagine the woman who grew up being hit every time she did something that her parents didn't like. She learned that the normal response to disobedience is physical. So when she has a child of her own and he misbehaves for the first time, her first inclination is to discipline him physically.

These are just some of the examples of the ways that the cycles from our childhood can seep into our life as adults. Creating these cycles is something that you do every day as a parent, right now. It's up to you to decide if this is going to be a good thing or a bad thing for your child. Your children are made in your image, literally. So why not give them something good to inherit.

We have this almost primary urge instilled in us to focus on things like wealth when we think about legacies for our children. This comes from the need to make sure that they don't struggle through life. If you look at generational cycles, you can see that the same idea can be applied. It's hard, and it is going to take work, but give your child the gift of not having to heal from your traumas.

OUTSIDE STRESSORS

Unfortunately, it isn't just the actions in the home that we need to think about when we are looking at managing anger. As adults, we are under almost constant pressure from the outside world as well. The little nuances of everyday life can stack onto the already teetering responsibilities we have at home.

- **Finances**: In this day and age, even families that are bringing in two incomes can struggle with finances. It can be a constant balancing act, trying to figure out exactly what needs to be paid, and what is going to have to wait for the next check to come in. You might be worried about how you are going to afford the shoes that your child needs for school, the part the car needs to keep running, and how to keep food on the table and the lights on. Worrying about finances can undoubtedly contribute to feelings of anger and outbursts at home.

- **Work**: Pressures at work can be a huge contributor to feelings of frustration, stress, and anger. You might be struggling to meet deadlines, working with difficult supervisors, or just be in an industry that is volatile. Unfortunately for most of us, the pressure doesn't alleviate when we clock out at the end of the day. We carry it with us into the home. The stress can leave us irritable or cause us to isolate just to find a moment's rest.

- **Health**: Health conditions plague us as parents, and for a majority of us, we don't have the time or the motivation to visit a doctor regularly. Chronic aches and pains, or other symptoms of health conditions can leave us with less patience than we need to be able to deal with home life calmly.

- **Relationships**: Relationships with your spouse, co-workers, and friends can greatly affect your emotions. If these relationships are feeling strained, it is easy for this to seep into the home and contribute to emotional outbursts.

3

EXPRESSING ANGER

Generally, people express their anger in three different ways. They either deal with their anger by expressing it, suppressing it, or they do it calmly. Understanding the different ways to express your anger can help you gauge where you are now, as well as decide how you would like to express yourself in the future.

Expressing anger, depending on the way it is executed, could be a good or bad method of communicating anger. A person who expresses their anger through emotionally intelligent communication, is likely going to encourage positive outcomes to conflict. It takes mindful, intentional actions to be able to outwardly communicate your anger positively. It can be really easy to come off as disrespectful, mean or even aggressive if a person doesn't take care with their words and actions when expressing anger.

Then there are people who suppress when they are trying to deal with anger. This can actually be a healthy and functional method, if it is done the right way. You can choose to suppress the anger, and then channel the energy into something else. The expulsion of energy or emotion still acts as a release, but it isn't as harmful as expressing the anger might have been. Managing your anger this way can actually be very dangerous if it is mismanaged. The emotion and energy is going to find a way out, one way or another. If you aren't careful to give it somewhere to go, it will decide a course on its own. Suppressing anger ineffectively can lead to behaviors like hostility, pessimism, and passive-aggression. It can also have effects on your blood pressure and it can create mental health issues like depression.

Handling anger calmly takes control in a couple of different areas. You have to be mentally able to identify the problem, and its causes. You'll also need to be able to practice techniques that will help you to physically calm your body. A person that expresses anger calmly might practice breathing or meditation to ease their body and their mind, ensuring that they are able to communicate their needs effectively.

If you are here, we can venture to guess that you are not managing or expressing your anger calmly. It would be really helpful on your journey to identify exactly how you are expressing your anger now. Are you expressing it, suppressing it, or doing a mixture of the two?

At this point, you've taken a good look at who you are, what your triggers are, and at any emotional baggage you might be carrying from your own childhood. So, in a sense, you have a good idea of what is making you angry. It's also vital to understand how your anger manifests when your emotions are getting the best of you. This is essential for a few reasons.

The first reason is simple, it is going to give you a bit more awareness for the moments that it does manifest. If you know that yelling is how your anger comes out, you might recognize just a little bit earlier that it is happening.

Motivation is another reason knowing how our anger manifests is important. Honestly, it's going to suck a little bit, looking at yourself angry from the outside. You are going to see just how ugly it can be, how unacceptable it is. It is okay to feel discouraged when you see what your anger looks like. Remember to separate yourself from it, and when you are done sulking, let it light a fire under your butt. Let watching how your anger manifests now be a motivation.

If we don't know what we are fighting, we cannot create a plan of attack, and this is the last reason you need to know how your anger manifests. There are different ways to deal with different anger manifestations. Knowing gives us a better chance of success at finding something that works for us to combat the anger. Know your body, yourself, your triggers, and how your anger manifests, because knowing is half the battle.

Common manifestations of anger:

External:

- Yelling or raising your voice.

- Throwing objects.

- Cursing or screaming obscenities.

- Verbal abuse, degrading comments, name-calling.

- Physical abuse, hitting, punching, or slapping.

Internal:

- Isolating yourself from others

- Self-harm/cutting.

- Self-verbal abuse comments

- Denial of needs like food, water, rest

Passive:

- Not talking

- Sarcasm

- Ignoring others/giving the cold shoulder

Take a few minutes to sit with yourself and recognize how your anger shows up in your life. Knowing how you typically react can help to create a plan to avoid these negative behaviors and redirect them in a positive way.

I know that this can be a lot to take in, and that it can be emotionally exhausting to have to take a deep hard look at your childhood, your triggers, and at yourself. Unfortunately, there is no way around anger management issues. The only way to make things better, is to walk through it. You need to learn all of these little things about yourself and about anger so that you can make the change. What does the scenario from the beginning of this chapter look like after we have taken a deep dive into ourselves?

Put it into action:

You are going to recognize the first signs of anger when your heart begins to race after your child tells you no the first time. Let this be an alarm bell that tells you it might be time to take a figurative step back from the situation. Why is it actually bothering you in this moment, what is taking you out of the driver seat? We can't decide to change until we know why our behavior needs changing.

Maybe being told no bothers you because it doesn't feel good and steals a bit of control from you, but your child refusing to clean their plate is what really grinds your gears. Maybe you were the child who couldn't get up until they were done. If you can recognize at this moment that this stems from your childhood, you can look at it further. Is your child malnourished or deficient in certain vitamins? Are they regularly lacking in the variety of foods they eat?

Maybe this is an opportunity for you to recognize that you need to come up with a better plan for meals. Maybe this means next time you introduce the nutrients in a different way, making the vegetables into a sauce, or even just substituting with a vitamin. Or is it an internal battle, where you need to recognize your own trauma? Is this a time where you decide, I'm not going to let my past dictate my future, my child is healthy and I'm going to give us both grace.

In this scenario the no could be what the trigger is for you. Hearing it will be the cue for you that you are going to need to do something. If this is the case, and you recognize that your anger manifests physically, maybe you make a point to distance yourself from the child. Maybe for you this scenario looks like getting up, putting your hands behind your back, and stepping away from the child before you continue.

While the scenario is going to look different for most parents, there are a few takeaways that remain the same. Understanding yourself, your past, and your triggers, is going to give you an edge on the anger. It's going to give you a signal, an understanding, and ideally some time to think before you act.

HOW DOES MY ANGER AFFECT ME?

So, we know what anger is. We know that it's a biological response from our body to something that it doesn't like. We're also aware that there is a long, exhausting list of things that can contribute to our feelings of anger. We know that we are triggered, and that we are probably carrying some emotional damage from when we were children. Finances, work, our health, and the relationships around us can also leave us feeling angry and irritable. Outside of the way that we behave with our children, it's important to understand what the consequences of unmanaged anger can be.

Most of us can count a couple of ways that the anger coming from all of these things can affect us. After all, you wouldn't be here if you didn't think that your anger was causing issues in your life in one way or another. So, let's take a look at the different ways not managing our anger can affect us.

Short term effects:

- Headaches

- Heart palpitations

- Increase in blood pressure.

- Fatigue

- Emotional outbursts

Long term effects:

- High blood pressure

- Cardiovascular problems

- Digestive issues

- Anxiety

Anger is a healthy part of life, as are the other emotions that we experience daily. It only becomes a problem when it is ignored, misunderstood or mishandled. Understanding what causes it, and how we react to it helps us to mitigate its possible downfalls. We don't want to eliminate it, but we want to let it serve us the way it is supposed to. The idea is to get to a place of understanding with ourselves, where our anger can talk to us, instead of for us.

4

WHO IS MY CHILD?

Scenario:

You are sitting at a crowded restaurant with your family. Your child is sitting quietly and coloring with some crayons on a napkin beside you. You are enjoying the conversation, the food, and being able to spend time with your family. You look over and see a smudge of ketchup on your child's face, and without thinking you grab a napkin and wipe her face. She gets upset and you don't realize why, until you look down and see that she drew a picture on the napkin you used to wipe her face. You apologize, and you go back to talking. A few minutes pass and you wipe up a spot of ketchup on the table. Your child screams, stands up, and pushes the chair she was sitting in over. You pick the chair up feeling absolutely mortified and you grab her hand, scolding out the door and all the way home.

The parent in this story is me. My daughter was maybe four years old, and the behavior was completely out of sorts for her. I knew her, and I could not fathom why she would think it would be okay to THROW A CHAIR in a crowded restaurant. I was embarrassed because I knew that I taught her better. I knew that she knew better than to behave like that, especially in public.

Looking back now I will tell you that I didn't know her, not at that moment. All I knew as I yelled at her was that she embarrassed me. I knew that everyone in that restaurant, including my family, was judging me. So, I raised my voice as I shook my finger in her face and I told her that she was bad, and that she made everyone think that I was a bad mom too.

We are all here because our anger is getting the best of us, and because it is having an effect on our children. We have taken the time to figure out what the anger is, why it is happening to us, and what triggers it. If we are going to take the steps to change our relationship with our children, we have to know who they are as well. Having a good grasp on your child's personality, triggers, and maturity level can help manage your own anger. It's helpful because it means that we know what to expect from them, and if we know what to expect, we can plan.

Here's a hard truth that I had to learn in my anger management journey with my children, *IT'S NOT THEIR FAULT BUT IT'S BECOME THEIR PROBLEM.* I had to sit down and recognize that my issues had become their issues, and that I had somehow convinced myself that it was their fault. I thought that they were causing my anger because they were whining, crying, fighting, or choosing not to listen.

In reality, I was completely missing the mark. They were trying to communicate their emotions but hadn't been taught how to do so effectively or responsibly. They were engaging in healthy conflict with their siblings, not trying to piss me off. They were asserting independence, not being disrespectful. They had nothing to do with it, not really, it was me. I misunderstood them, because *I didn't know them* or myself.

KNOW YOUR CHILD'S PERSONALITY

A lack of understanding who our children are and why they behave the way they do, can leave us unprepared to deal with them calmly and with empathy. It's hard to be able to sit down and say I am the problem. I could have planned our day better. I could have spoken in words they would understand. I could have set this boundary and enforced it.

A lot of us spent months during our pregnancies wondering who our children are going to become, what they are going to be like, and then life happens. Somewhere between the diapers and tantrums we forget to keep looking, and to keep learning. So, let's take a look at some of the personality and character traits that will help you understand your child a little better.

- **Curiosity**: How curious is your child? Do they like to explore the unknown or does something outside of their comfort zone make them feel anxious and afraid?

- **Courage**: Does your child like to push the limits and see how far they can go? Do they enjoy the monkey bars, even if they might fall ten times before they can get across? Does your child pull away from things that could hurt them, emotionally or physically? Are they afraid to try new things or new foods because they are fine right where they are?

- **Patience**: What is your child's patience level like? How long does it take for them to start losing it in a grocery store, or when they are waiting for you to make their favorite snack?

- **Adaptability**: Is routine important for your child? Do they like to stray from the normal day to day activities or do they feel better when they know bath time is at seven and bedtime is at eight?

- **Confidence**: How confident is your child in themselves and their abilities? Do they need a pep talk before the first day of school or do they want to invite the whole class to their birthday party?

- **Resilience**: How easy is it for your child to struggle and overcome a problem? Do they want to give up after the first try or are they going to keep going until they get it right?

- **Empathy**: How well does your child share in other people's feelings? It is hard for them to see how they affect someone else with their actions or is it easy for you to explain your feelings to your child and have them understand what you mean?

If you take the time to learn a bit more about your child, it is going to make your life easier. Most of us have some idea already. We dread bedtime because we know that our child is going to do everything they can to avoid it. We prepare ourselves before a doctor's appointment, because we know our child is going to cry if they get even an inkling that they might have to receive a shot. When you gain a better understanding, you can change your approach to uncomfortable situations that involve your child. One small change can make a world of difference when you already feel like you are hanging from a thread emotionally.

Put it into action:

Your child is learning to ride a bike, and you think it is time for the training wheels to come off, so you are taking them to the park for lunch and to practice.

The Resilient Child: You know your child doesn't have a problem scraping his knees and getting back up. You're going to take the training wheels off of the bike and be there when they need you to kiss their knee and make it feel better. You are going to watch them fall, and get back on and try again.

The Non-Resilient Child: You know your child struggles with failure. They are easily frustrated and give up quickly. You are going to take a little bit longer to take the training wheels off of their bike. When you do take them off, you're going to hold onto the seat for a little bit longer. If they want to quit, you are going to have a pep talk ready for them. If that doesn't work you have a candy bar in your back pocket to get them to the finish line. You're going to walk into the situation knowing that if all else fails you are going to try again another day.

If you try to push the non-resilient child, knowing what they are like, you are probably going to run into some sort of negative behavior. There is also an added chance that whatever negative behavior they show is going to make you angry. Planning around the child, instead of making them fit your plans is going to help you avoid conflict.

Where your child measures with all of these different personality and character traits tells you a lot about who they are. It's not up to us as parents to judge our children, or to try to mold them how we'd like. It's up to us to meet them where they are. Knowing your child in this sense makes it easier for you to help them manage their behaviors. As parents, we all know that if we had a little bit more control over our children, it would be that much easier for us to manage our own emotions.

When we talk about knowing our children, personality and character are just the tip of the iceberg. Their triggers, age, maturity level, and ability to regulate emotionally are going to change how we interact with our children as well. What works for a five-year-old is not going to work for your teenager.

TRIGGERED CHILDREN, TRIGGER PARENTS

You've already taken a hard look at the things that triggered you. This gives you an advantage because knowing what your triggers are can help you avoid them. You can plan your daily life in a way that minimizes your risk of being emotionally overwhelmed by something that really bothers you. It's also important that you take the time to identify your child's triggers. Because let's be honest, for most of us parents, our children being triggered happens to be our biggest trigger.

When something upsets your child, and they are struggling with their own anger, they tend to act out. This can look different for every child, but the reactionary behaviors are rarely good. More than likely, your child showing these behaviors is just going to further stress you out. When the world seems like it is falling apart and nothing can ever just go right, the last thing a stressed and struggling parent needs is a tantrum. So here are some things that might be triggering your child:

- Parental anger

- Lack of sleep

- Sickness

- Being hungry

- Loud noises

- Crowds

- Bullying

- Homework frustrations

- Social circle frustrations

These are just a few things that can be a negative trigger for your child. Paying attention to what happens directly before an outburst or change in behavior from your child is going to be key in identifying your child's specific triggers. Once you have taken the time to really get to know who your child is, and what trigger's negative behaviors in them, you are better able to come up with a plan to avoid their emotional outbursts.

If we look back at the scenario from the beginning of this chapter, I can once again tell you that in those moments, I did not know my child. I knew exactly how she was making me feel, I knew exactly what I felt like she did wrong, but I didn't take *her* into account. If I had, I guarantee that I would not have acted out in anger afterwards. So, what I have learned about my daughter since that incident is this:

- She is creative: When I used the napkin, I destroyed something that mattered to her and something that she was proud of.

- She is highly emotional, more so than any of my other children: When I used the napkin for the first time, it meant a lot of things to her. It meant she did not matter, that I did not care about her feelings and I'm sure a list of other things. She has a short fuse and could not emotionally handle the same thing happening again so quickly.

- She lacks confidence and because of that she looks for approval from others outside of herself. She needs praise from others to feel loved. She wanted to be able to show me that picture, and hear me tell her how beautiful it was, and instead I destroyed it.

- She is triggered when she does not feel heard. When I ignored her the first time I hurt her feelings, even though I apologized. I did not listen actively to what she was saying with her words or with her body language. If I were actively listening, I would have been mindful enough to not do it again.

- Her outlet for emotional overload is sometimes physical: When she feels overwhelmed with anger, and even other emotions, she reacts physically. This could mean throwing something, hitting something/someone, or just stomping away.

So here is what I would do now, after learning about her personality, adjusting my expectations for her age, and knowing her triggers.

Ideally in this situation I would not have reached for the napkin to wipe her face in the first place, but I did. So, we can start there, after the initial conflict. I'm going to put myself in her shoes, empathize, and realize the gravity of how I hurt her. I'm going to imagine making her a picture, and then watching her destroy it. I'm going to recognize that she is probably feeling a mixture of different emotions, sadness, disappointment, and anger.

I will disengage from the conversation at the table totally, get down to a level where I can see her eye to eye, and I'm going to genuinely apologize. I'm going to acknowledge how she feels verbally, telling her that I understand that she is feeling hurt, sad, and probably a little bit mad at me. After this, I am going to take the time to give her my undivided attention. Maybe I will color with her, or just comment on her work as she draws. Knowing what I know now about my child, I would not make the mistake of doing it a second time. I would spend the rest of the dinner gauging where she is emotionally, and holding space so that she feels valued and seen.

HOW DO I AFFECT MY CHILD?

We learned a lot about our children in the last chapter. We took a look at who they are, and what triggers negative behaviors in them. We talked about how their negative behaviors can actually cause emotional outbursts for us. Now, we are going to take a deep, hard look at what a lack of anger management from us can do to them.

This chapter might be hard for you, and in truth, it should be. None of us parents want to hurt our children, but the reality is that we do, and that is supposed to bother us. Those of us who struggle with anger, tend to hurt them more often than we'd like. The actions we take, and the ones we don't, have an immediate and lasting impact on them. It's important to understand this without letting it discourage you. You've made mistakes, but you are here, you are learning, and you aren't going to give up.

If there is one singular way to apologize for all of the collective times that you've taken your anger out on your children, it's to make the change.

Even when our anger as parents is gone the effects can linger in the echoes of the home. Children often bear the brunt of these emotional storms. They are impressionable and are constantly learning from the interactions they see around them. The presence of anger, especially when it is recurring, can leave permanent marks on their emotional and psychological health.

Emotional Development

In the earliest stages of life, children are like sponges, they soak up everything. The only proof you need here is that one time you accidentally said a bad word, and they repeated it for weeks afterwards. They learn by watching, especially in the early years when that is the only way they know how to learn. So, we know that the tone we set in the home is going to influence them, but how exactly? The way we behave, how we react to the spilled milk, or the messy room is going to show our children how they are supposed to manage their own emotions. Repeated exposure to anger can damage this understanding, fostering an environment where emotions such as fear, sadness, or anxiety may dominate.

Children look to their parents as models for how to navigate their feelings. If they see that anger is the go-to reaction to stress or conflict, they are going to see it as normal. This modeling can hinder their ability to explore a range of emotional responses and express them appropriately. Children cannot learn what they do not see. If you are unable to handle your emotions in a healthy way, they will not be able to either.

It's also worth noting children need to witness the full spectrum of emotions, including anger, to develop robust emotional intelligence. It's the context and frequency that tip the scales. So, what does this mean for parents? We need to show them anger, they are going to experience it in the world. They need to see us angry, and then they need to see what tools we use to work through it calmly and compassionately.

Behavioral Mimicry

Children are adept at mirroring the behaviors they see. It is how a child learns how to walk, talk, and eat. The same principle applies to expressing emotions. If a parent's anger results in slammed doors or raised voices, it shouldn't come as a surprise when a child exhibits similar behaviors.

This mimicry isn't merely imitation for its own sake; it's a learning mechanism through which children develop their behaviors. They test out responses they've seen, gauging the outcomes and then they adjust to what works for them. When the modeled behavior is anger, it can lead to a pattern of aggressive responses to their own experiences of frustration or disappointment.

Moreover, these behaviors can seep into their interactions outside the home. A child who learns anger is an acceptable response to irritation might have a hard time during conflicts with peers. They might not understand why the other children don't want to play with them when they yell. The child could struggle to form friendships, which could lead to issues with self-confidence, or they could also be labeled as "troubled' or difficult".

Long-term Psychological Effects

The long-term psychological effects of consistent exposure to parental anger can follow a child for life. Research shows children who grow up in environments where anger is frequently expressed are at higher risk for a variety of mental health challenges, including depression, anxiety, and low self-esteem. This can be hard to keep in the forefront of your mind when you are lost in your emotions. The idea here is to let the possible implications of your anger be a source of motivation.

There is also an added risk that the child may begin to believe that they are to blame for the anger, and they aren't, not really. You aren't to blame for it either, we learned this when we looked at our own childhoods and triggers. The only caveat here is that you can do something about it, you can understand and utilize tools to change it. Your child can't do that unless someone models it for them. Children can misconstrue their parent's anger and this, with their egocentric view of the world, can misconstrue the source of their parents' anger. The child might start to believe the anger is a direct result of their own actions or existence. This can lead to a fragile sense of self-worth.

Stress induced by a volatile emotional environment can impact cognitive functioning, which is just another way of saying it can affect the way their brain works. Chronic stress in childhood has been linked to difficulties in learning, memory, and attention. The brain is so busy with managing emotional turmoil that it can't process and retain new information.

It's also important to consider a child's future parenting style may be shaped by early experiences. The patterns learned in childhood often resurface when we become parents ourselves. How many generational cycles did you come up with in the beginning of the book? What cycles are you creating for your children? People tend to fall back on what they know, so it is important to address and change any unhealthy behaviors surrounding anger now.

While the impact of anger on children can be profound, it's never too late to shift the dynamics within a family. Is it going to be perfect? No, because nothing in life ever is. But it can be more peaceful, more joyful, and more hopeful. Parents can take steps to lessen the effects of past anger and create a more supportive environment moving forward. The best way to do this is think about how you react to anger and find a way to cope that you would be happy with your child mimicking.

For parents who recognize the need for change, the road ahead is filled with opportunities for growth and healing. It will be filled with days where you might feel like you didn't do enough, and there will absolutely be days where you lose your cool. But here's the thing, there will be moments that make it all worth it. There's going to be a time at the dinner table, or doing homework, or in the grocery store where you see the difference. You are going to take the deep breath or respond in empathy, and you will feel renewed. Vindicated against the anger that could have consumed you, if you had let it.

It requires commitment, self-exploration and the courage to adopt new approaches. By doing so, not only can the cycle of anger be disrupted, but a foundation for emotional well-being and resilience can be built for both you and your child. Committing to the change means healing your relationship with your child and disrupting the cycle of anger.

It's essential to hold onto the vision of the kind of home we want as we look at the changes we need to make. One where emotions are expressed healthily, where children feel safe and valued. Keep the picture of the home where they are able to grow and thrive happily in the forefront of your mind. Imagine a time and place where you are able to move through your day without the guilt of an accidental outburst.

5

BENEFITS OF CHANGING

There are parts of this chapter that are probably going to make you really excited to make a change because managing anger can change your life in monumental ways. It can help with your physical and mental health. It will also have a direct impact on your relationships, in and outside of the home. The most important one, the one that probably brought you here in the first place, is that it will have a positive impact on your child.

- **Physical**

Long term unmanaged anger can wreak havoc on your body. Decreasing the amount of anger and stress in your life can lessen these effects. You could be less likely to develop high blood pressure, have a stroke, or have heart disease. Incorporating exercise into your self-care routines can also boost the physical benefits of managing anger.

- **Mental**

We all know the toll it takes on us as parents when we give in to emotional outbursts. Taking steps to manage the anger can help you avoid issues like anxiety, depression, guilt, and high stress levels. It can also give your self-esteem a boost. Anger management techniques can help you feel more in control and more aligned with your values and life goals.

- **Relationships**

Working on your anger can have a huge impact on your relationships, even those outside of your children. A majority of the techniques taught in this book are aimed at getting you more in tune with yourself and your emotions. The benefits of this will touch a number of different parts of your life. You would be able to communicate your emotions better, which will allow your spouse, friends, and family to develop deeper connections to you. You will be better able to handle conflicts in and out of the home, which may even make your work life a bit easier.

- **For my child**

Here's the reality. Children who live in homes where anger is ever present are hurting, even if it doesn't show. The list of ways your anger can affect them now and in the future is endless. Luckily, you are here, and it's not too late. Making a change now, even a small one, can have a positive impact on their lives. Just by being here and taking the first step, you are on the road to doing these things for your child:

Improve Their Self-Image: Managing anger means giving your child a better outlook on who they are as a person. They are less likely to blame your emotional outbursts on their actions, or even just their existence, which will obviously make them feel better about themselves. They will think they are better, more deserving people than they think they are now. This can lead to healthier interactions in relationships later on in life. They will require more respect, love, and empathy from others because they know they deserve it.

Encourage Self-Regulation: You are going to teach your child a better way to handle their own emotions when you work to manage your anger. They will have an easier time in social situations, with their own relationships in the future, and with their own children someday. Changing the pattern now means rewriting the script for them.

Encourage Empathy and Emotional Intelligence: Watching you practice empathy is going to help your child. Teaching your children what you have learned about your emotions and the emotions of the people around you is going to have a profound effect on them. They will build their own relationships on a more solid foundation. They will be more compassionate, loving, giving people just by watching you model the behaviors for them.

Improve Grades: Anger in the home can affect cognitive abilities, remember? This means that your child will likely have an easier time in school just because you have decided to take steps towards managing your anger. This could give them a better chance at furthering their education, and finding a career that makes them feel fulfilled.

Decrease The Risk of Mental Health issues: Managing your anger at home can decrease the risk of your child having to struggle with things like anxiety and depression in the future.

Improve Their Relationship with You: This is important. Deciding to make the change, will change your relationship with your child forever. As parents, there is nothing in the world we love more than our children. It is instinctive, and ingrained. Anger can sometimes make it hard for us and for our children to see that. It can build a wall that can seem insurmountable for your child to climb. Managing your anger is going to bring you closer to your child, it's going to help close the gap. It's going to create opportunities for genuine, natural, beautiful moments that you both will carry with you for the rest of your lives.

6

MAKING THE CHANGE: MOTIVATION

Everyone is motivated differently but people rarely commit to a change without a reason. You need motivation, a reason to keep going when your energy is gone and you just don't feel like doing the work. As parents, it can be really easy to give in to whatever works in the moment. You are stressed and you are just trying to keep the peace and live to see another day.

Something is going to have to speak to you, something is going to have to be able to get through to you. So what is going to work for you, what is going to keep you motivated and committed to making the changes, no matter how hard they get? Wanting to change your anger for your child is probably what brought you here, but what is going to keep you here?

Before you begin to make changes, you need to know why you are making them. Take a look at the list above and at yourself. Dig deep to find the motivation, and then make it visible. Write it in a journal, on your phone, or maybe on the fridge. Put it somewhere you are going to see it, read it, and be able to pull resiliency from it.

At this point, we've learned a ton, and if you are anything like me, things could be getting cloudy. So, before we continue on to exactly how to make the change let's recap:

Anger is normal, and while it won't go away completely, it is not you, and it can be controlled. Anger is a biological response your body has, to something that it doesn't like. If you pay close enough attention, your body will give you signals when it is getting ready to blow. Your personality, triggers, past, and outside stressors can all contribute to anger if you let them. Depending on who you are, an overflow of anger is going to manifest itself differently. One universal truth is that it is going to affect you, your health, relationships, and your child. You can improve your mental health, physical health, and relationships if you follow through on your commitment to learn to control your anger.

Now, you have a better understanding of anger, and why it's important to *you* to change. Together we are going to walk through making things happen. Forgiveness, self-care, emotional intelligence, communication, pauses, breathing, and boundaries are going to be your tools. Let's get started.

7

MAKING THE CHANGE: PRACTICE FORGIVENESS

Forgiveness is powerful, it is freeing, and you need to give it and receive it to begin healing. So many of us parents harbor resentment, and don't recognize the profound effect it has on us, and how we treat our children. If you want to be able to stop letting your anger win, you need to learn to forgive others, and most importantly *yourself.*

When we forgive, we are not agreeing with or dismissing the wrongs of the past. Rather, we are acknowledging them and choosing to release their grip on us. Forgiveness is hard, but it can transform the energy of anger into a force for healing and growth.

FORGIVENESS AS A TOOL FOR ANGER MANAGEMENT

The act of forgiveness is an internal and conscious decision to let go of negative emotions. When we harbor anger, it often manifests in parenting. Sometimes in subtle ways—a sharp tone, an impatient gesture, a reluctance to engage. By choosing forgiveness, we clear away these barriers, opening a path to more genuine and loving interactions with our children.

Forgiveness also serves to model; it shows a powerful lesson for our children that everyone makes mistakes, and it is possible to move beyond them with compassion and empathy. Learning forgiveness can improve the way a child interacts with those around them and help them to mature emotionally. This lesson can resonate deeply, influencing their own social interactions and emotional maturity.

Steps to Forgiving Self and Others

Forgiveness is a journey that begins with a single, often difficult step, acknowledging that you are hurting. Here are steps that can guide you through the process:

- **Reflect on the Hurt**: What traumas from your past are you still holding on to. Consider how holding onto anger has affected you. Look back on how it has changed your relationships with the people around you and your parent-child relationships. Think of the specific incidents or patterns contributing to this anger.

Example: Reflect on the times that you have let anger get the best of you, and your children have suffered for it. Think about the pain it caused you and them, when the adrenaline was gone, and you were left with only your thoughts.

- **Empathize with the Offender**: Try to understand the circumstances or motivations behind the actions that caused you pain. This is not about excusing the behavior but seeing it from a different point of view. It is not always going to be easy or even possible to empathize, depending on the offense. If this step does not work for you, continue on to the next.

Example: Empathize with yourself, understand that you were suffering from wounds you didn't know how to heal, and that you didn't have the tools you needed to get better.

- **Decide to Forgive:** Make the conscious decision to forgive, recognizing this is for your emotional well-being as much as for healing relationships. Understand that this *forgiveness is not consent* *for the behavior to continue.* <u>Sorry means changed behavior</u>, and if you've received an apology, hold the person accountable for that.

Example: You need to decide to forgive yourself. Make room for something else to grow in the space you've allocated for anger, shame, and guilt. Recognize that you were wrong, that you don't allow the behavior anymore, and that you are going to change it.

- **Express Your Forgiveness:** You can choose to communicate your forgiveness to the person who wronged you. You can do this directly or through a symbolic gesture, such as writing a letter and then ripping it up to represent releasing the anger.

Example: My anger is, but it isn't me. I forgive myself for letting it hurt me and the people around me. I acknowledge the mistakes I've made and understand that perfection is an impossible standard. I grant myself the same grace I would offer to others.

- **Transform Your Insight into Action:** Use what you have learned to change your behavior going forward. Apologize for your mistakes and commit to using forgiveness moving forward. Use your understanding to inform your future behavior. Make amends where necessary and commit to patterns of interaction that reflect your forgiveness.

Example: I have made mistakes, and let anger cause me to behave in ways that go against my intentions and morals. I am actively taking steps to change this and commit to a better version of myself. I can give myself compassion and forgiveness while also holding myself accountable.

- **Seek Closure:** Find a way to mark the act of forgiveness, whether it's through a conversation, a moment of quiet reflection, or a ritual that holds personal significance.

Example: Make it personal. This is about you. The change will affect others, of course, but it is about you. How are you going to give yourself the gift of forgiveness?

As it is, forgiveness is not easy. It can be even harder if you cannot communicate with the person that hurt you. These ideas might be helpful for the less simple violations we need to learn to forgive and let go:

- Get a piece of paper and write down whatever it is you are trying to forgive or let go. Express how it made you feel, and how it affected you in the long term or the short term. Let yourself feel it, and live in the emotions for a moment (this is a good time to cry it out if you need to). Now let it go, bury it, rip it up, whatever works for you, but let it go.

- Grab a canvas and a paintbrush. Use words, pictures, or even just scribbles to symbolize the pain or emotions you want to expel. Again, let yourself feel it for a moment, tune into it. When you are done, imagine your life without that pain, imagine the freedom of letting it go, and paint what that feels like to you.

THE FREEDOM OF LETTING GO

Letting go is the essence of forgiveness. It is making room for positive interactions with our children and those around us. It is choosing to focus our attention and intentions on what we can do instead of what has already been done. It helps us to make an environment where love and happiness can flourish.

It's the act of unclenching the fist of anger to extend an open hand instead. In the context of parenting, letting go can rejuvenate the joy and spontaneity that anger may have dampened and reclaim that energy. This newfound energy can be redirected into positive interactions with our children, fostering an environment where your family is free to be themselves.

Letting go is not a one-time event. It's a practice, a repeated choice we make in life. It is a commitment to maintaining an open heart, even when we are triggered. This not only transforms our parenting but teaches our children the value of emotional freedom and the skillset to achieve it.

Embracing forgiveness is like tending a garden. It requires patience and care. Just as we pull weeds to prevent them from choking the life from our plants, so too must we weed out resentment to allow love to prosper. *This act is an affirmation of our capacity for change and our unwavering commitment to our family's well-being.*

Your Review Can Spark Change

Embrace the Joy of Giving

"Every act of kindness creates a ripple with no logical end." - Scott Adams

Did you know that when you lend a hand or share a kind word, you help others and bring more joy and friendship into your life? So, if we have a chance to spread a little kindness, let's grab it with both hands!

I've got a small request for you...

Would you consider offering a helping hand to someone you've never met, even if you don't get anything back?

Who are we talking about? Someone very much like you. Someone who is trying their best to improve, looking for a guiding light but unsure where to find it.

We're on a mission to make the journey of mastering anger as a parent accessible to all. Everything we do is driven by this purpose. To achieve our goal, we need to reach out to...basically everyone.

That's where your help is invaluable. It turns out reviews really matter when it comes to choosing a book. So, on behalf of parents who are in the thick of it, just as you may be, here's what I'm asking:

Could you take a moment to leave a review for this book?

This simple act requires no money and just a minute of your time, yet it could profoundly impact another parent's life. Your review could be the nudge that helps.

...a family find harmony.

...a parent learn patience and understanding.

...another person build a stronger bond with their children.

...a dream of a calm and loving household come to light.

To spread this kindness and truly make a difference, all it takes is a moment to...

write a review.

Zap the QR COde right here to share your thoughts:

If the idea of helping another parent warms your heart, then you're exactly who we love to have around here. Welcome to the community. You're a part of something wonderful.

I'm thrilled to guide you through new approaches to managing emotions, enhancing communication, and fostering a nurturing home with greater ease than you imagined. The techniques and insights in the next chapters are sure to be game-changers.

Thank you from the bottom of my heart. Now, let's continue on this important journey together.

- Your biggest supporter, T. Nicole.

8

MAKING THE CHANGE: SELF-CARE

I know, I know. Time for yourself can seem like a joke when you are struggling with a job, homework, dinner, and tantrums. You've barely got enough time in a day as it is, and somehow, you're supposed to find time to pamper yourself? Well, YES! Self-care is going to be your most important tool in anger management. It keeps you in tune with your emotions, helps align your actions with your intentions, and it helps soothe your nerves. If we have learned anything thus far, it's that our nerves NEED soothing. Sometimes it feels like the universe aligns just to get on our nerves, so we need to cushion them.

When you make a commitment to care for yourself and your well-being, you are inadvertently committing to being a better parent. Have you heard the saying, "You can't pour from an empty cup?" Well, in terms of parenting, truer words might never have been uttered. *You cannot give your child peace if you do not have it. You cannot give them comfort if you don't know what it feels like.* Your capacity to share love, joy, and empathy will get better if you commit to yourself and your self-care.

PRIORITIZING SELF-CARE

Are you going to be able to dedicate a full hour to making yourself happy? Probably not. It's the small commitments you make during the day that are going to make the change for you.

Before we get too far into this, it is vital to understand that caring for yourself is not selfish, and it is not negotiable, not if you want to efficiently manage your anger. It's in our nature as parents to give. If you are full of anger, resentment, and stress, it is going to bleed into your children. If you take the time to fill yourself with hope, and joy, and happiness, well you get the idea. Here are some helpful tools to help prioritize and manage your time.

- **Calendar Integration:** You've likely got play-dates, soccer games, and red-shirt days neatly marked on your calendar for your children. It's time to do the same for yourself. Mark space on your calendar for self-care where you can. Collaborate with your partner and communicate with your children about these times.

- **Micro-Moments**: Realistically, there isn't going to always be a whole day that you can take for yourself. Sometimes, the emotional outburst is a minute away and you need something right now. Self-care doesn't always have to be lengthy. You might need to leave your child waiting for five minutes before you start a bedtime story for some self-care. That's okay, it's going to pay off in the long run.

- **Negotiables and Non-Negotiables:** Time management is essential here, but so is knowing what can wait, and what cannot. The dishes can wait, but your emotional outburst wont. Figure out what your non-negotiables are, and plan accordingly. By the way Momma/Daddy, your self-care is non-negotiable!

ADAPTING SELF-CARE PRACTICES TO PERSONAL NEEDS

We've spent a lot of time talking about children, and how parental anger can affect them. The focus here though, needs to be on you. Self-care is deeply personal. If you are not a creative person, making time for painting or sketching isn't going to serve you. If I know that I need self-care time, I'm not going for a jog. Is it good for me? Yes, but it has its time and place, which doesn't happen to be during MY self-care. Where does your joy come from, what makes you feel exhilarated or fulfilled?

Picture the worst day you can imagine. The kids are all in full gremlin mode, the house is a mess, work was suffocating, and Murphy's law has been the name of the game all day long. What do you need in this moment, when you are two seconds from absolutely losing it, and you just feel like giving up? What is going to give you enough gusto to make it to bedtime without adding on the guilt of an emotional outburst aimed at your child? Make sure it makes sense, make sure it's manageable, and make sure it's for you.

- **Know yourself:** If you only have five minutes to make yourself feel better, know what is going to make a difference. Is it a cup of tea, a walk, meditation etc. Do a little bit of soul searching to make sure you aren't expending energy (that none of us parents have) on something that isn't going to help.

- **Self-Assessment:** You should have daily interactions with yourself. You aren't always going to need the same thing. Today you might need a few minutes to yourself, and tomorrow you might need to feel a deeper connection to your spouse, or your children. Be ready to change self-care techniques to give you what you need.

- **Seasonal Adjustments:** As the seasons change, our self-care needs and practices are going to change. Bright summer mornings might invite an outdoor jog, while winter evenings could be perfect for a few chapters of your favorite book by the fire.

- **Life's Ebb and Flow:** Be willing to modify your self-care routine in response to life's fluctuations. During particularly hectic weeks, simplify practices to maintain consistency without adding pressure. Have a backup plan. Your favorite songs loaded to a self-care playlist, an emergency stash of Oreos, or even a small pre-bought gift that can help lift your spirit.

INCORPORATING SELF-CARE INTO DAILY LIFE

We know it's not always easy to incorporate self-care into our daily life. There are small things that you can do, to encourage yourself to take the time. What are your excuses for not being able to practice self-care, and what are the solutions.

- **Family Involvement**: Involve your children in self-care activities when appropriate. If you can't find time away from the children in the moment, build your self-care around them. Cooking a healthy meal together turns a chore into a bonding activity and teaches valuable life skills. Hand your child a paint brush, a book, or even a face mask. Do what you have to, to feel more like yourself. More than once I've had to involve my children, and then studiously pretend that they weren't there to get in some self-care.

- **Ritual Attachment:** If you are short on time, link self-care practices to existing habits. While brushing your teeth, practice gratitude, or recite affirmations. While showering, you can visualize washing away the stress.

- **Environment Design:** Craft your environment to encourage self-care. A basket of books by your favorite chair invites reading, and a yoga mat in the corner beckons a stretch. These visual prompts remind you to take care of yourself amidst the daily bustle.

Once you have figured out what is going to work for you, and how you are going to incorporate it into daily life.

Put it into action:

Consistency and awareness is key here. Know yourself and give yourself grace when you need it. Here are some other ways you can practice self-care:

When you have time for yourself:

- Go for a walk or get some sun. Life can be suffocating, especially when you are a stressed parent. Let yourself breathe, and just be.

- Plant a garden, or some flowers. Getting in touch with nature can be so healing for the mind, body, and soul.

- Paint/Color/Doodle, let yourself get in touch with the creative parts of you, or even just with your inner child.

- Read a book.

- Start a journal and give yourself an outlet for pent up emotions, or even just a place to jot down your hopes and dreams.

- Pamper yourself, get a massage, a haircut or get your nails done.

- Go shopping, buy a new fishing rod, a new pair of shoes, or just get out of the house for a bit.

- Get a hobby, or maybe just cultivate your skills with a new one. Start sewing or playing basketball.

- Dance

- Skip cooking and order out, use the extra time to get in touch with yourself or just relax.

- Make a kind gesture, sometimes giving something to someone else can be the best medicine.

- Listen to music or a podcast.

- Have a bath, bubbles and all.

Child Friendly Self-care:

- Cook together WITHOUT worrying about the mess. Get flour everywhere, and laugh about it.

- Watch a movie together, in a fort surrounded by pillows and fluffy blankets.

- Do a puzzle or crush your children in your favorite board game.

- Make a gratitude list.

- Make smores and stargaze.

- Have a dance party but PLEASE watch the coatrack.

- Take a walk or go for a bike ride.

Scenario:

You are doing homework with your children, and one problem seems to be taking twenty minutes to finish. Your child is fidgeting, sighing, and doing anything BUT their homework. You worked all day, and you are feeling drained, and you are ready to give up. You know that homework is important, and so you push. You try to explain why it's important, you tell them that if they just focus it will go faster, you try to bribe them with something sweet. Nothing works.

This was me, just a couple of months ago. My patience was almost non-existent. My child was struggling in school, and I had this narrative in my head that it was my fault. I wanted to be the mom that finished the homework AND got to go through the flashcards with her child. I wanted to know that I was making a difference for my daughter. No matter what I did at that moment, she just would not focus on her work. I was jabbing the pencil at her paper and could tell that all of my frustration was just looking for somewhere to go.

At that moment, something clicked. It wasn't going to happen, the homework was not getting done, not then at least. I had no patience, I needed a break, and she needed to do anything other than stare at that paper and feel like she was failing me. I got up, walked into my room, grabbed a pair of underwear and put them on my head. Yes, you read that right, on my head. I put socks on my hands, tied a bra around my butt, turned some music on, grabbed my daughter and we danced.

The homework never did get finished, and I actually broke my toe doing the Cha Cha Slide directly into the coat rack. That is not the moral of this scenario though. I needed self-care at that moment. I needed to be freed of the constraints of work and the worries of being a bad mom. She needed to feel like there was more to our relationship than homework, and healthy balanced dinners.

Homework is easier now. I know to listen to myself and to my daughter. We still struggle but now I know that paying attention pays off. I know to give us a few minutes to care for ourselves when we need it. Most days the homework gets done, and neither of us feels so crappy about it anymore.

The lesson here is not that self-care is going to fix everything, because it won't. You will still blow up, and some days will be worse than others. But if you take the time to give yourself grace, it will make changes in your life. Sometimes the smallest changes lift the most weight from your shoulders. Here are some other ways practicing self-care can help with anger:

Improved Emotional Regulation

The small moments that we take for self-care, strengthen the bond we have with ourselves, and our emotions. We are in a better position to really be able to hear our mind and body as they speak to us. Being able to regulate our emotions more efficiently can improve our overall lives in so many ways. Most importantly, it puts you in a better position to manage your anger. With that being said, here are some other ways to help improve your emotional regulation skills with self-care:

- **Emotional Check-ins:** Create a routine of checking in on yourself and your emotions. This can be as simple as asking, "How am I feeling right now?" during a lunch break or while the kids are doing homework. This one small addition to your day can help catch any negative emotions from evolving into something that is unmanageable.

- **Creative Outlets**: Do activities that channel emotions constructively. Painting, gardening, or playing an instrument are not just hobbies; they are vents for pent-up emotions. If you find yourself facing uncomfortable emotions during a check in, don't give them an opportunity to fester. Confront them and release them, it can be really fun if you let it be.

Enhanced Patience

In parenting, patience is needed to deal with daily challenges. Self-care strengthens this ability, no matter what awaits. Self-care in its essence brings us clarity, and a sense of peace. It gives us resilience, and armor against the day's frustrations. Here are some self-care practices that can help with patience:

- Don't forget to extend thanks for the good things that happen. Celebrate the little moments. This reflection turns the mind towards the positive, elongating the fuse of patience.

- Start a project with the family, that everyone can take a turn with. For example, a collage. Have everyone choose pictures of a moment in time that means something to them. Each family member can take turns adding to the collage and communicating their feelings. This can help foster patience, but it can also strengthen emotional bonds between all of you.

- Print a piece of paper with the word patience on it. You can place it on the homework table or give it to your children when they are sharing turns with a toy. You can use it when you need to remember to be patient with your child when they are struggling. Your children can use it to remind them to be patient with each other when they are playing.

By nurturing patience through self-care, we cultivate understanding and compassion, allowing us to meet our children's needs with a calmness that speaks louder than words.

THE IMPACT OF SELF-CARE ON PARENTING

Increased Emotional Resilience

Parenthood represents a circle of emotions: joy, frustration, triumph, anger, and love. Emotional resilience holds it all together. This resilience allows parents to sway with the gusts of day-to-day life without breaking. Self-care, and even this book, is not going to fix everything. You are going to have bad days. Giving yourself time, compassion, and consideration just makes it a little easier to get through the bad days.

- **Adaptability in the Face of Adversity:** You will find that you have a renewed sense of strength and flexibility when you practice self-care. You are better equipped, mentally and physically rested, and ready to take on whatever the world decides to throw at you.

- **Quicker Recovery from Setbacks:** Just as a well-maintained vehicle can weather a long journey more effectively, a parent who prioritizes their well-being can bounce back more swiftly from the inevitable setbacks of parenting. They can emerge stronger, with learned wisdom from each experience. When you walk into a conflict with your child in a stable state of mind because you are taking care of yourself, you are better able to take care of them.

Improved Parent-Child Relationship

When parents partake in self-care they bring a presence to their parent-child interactions that isn't clouded with exhaustion. How many times have you played dolls, board games, or listened to your child talk about their day without actually being mentally present. Self-care is going to help you make the small moments count. As a parent who can never find enough time in a day, feeding into yourself can help you make even the smallest moments worth remembering. Being more in tune with yourself, and practicing looking for signs of inner turmoil will also help you guide your children through times of adversity.

- **Presence and Attunement:** With the clarity self-care provides, parents can attune themselves more precisely to their children's needs and emotions. They can pick up on the subtle cues, the unspoken words, and the needs that lie beneath the surface, responding with a sensitivity that fosters deep connection. As humans, we all feel more loved when we feel understood. Practicing self-care can help you give this understanding to your children.

- **Consistent Loving Engagement**: Children flourish under the steady light of attention and love. Self-care ensures parents can offer this consistency, even when external pressures mount. The energy reserves built through self-care translate into an ability to engage lovingly with children, even at the end of a long day.

Enhanced Ability to Model Healthy Habits

Children are impressionable, we know that they love to mimic what they are seeing. It shows when they make a new friend, or when they get a new teacher. It will also show when you begin to change the pattern of your behaviors. When self-care is a visible part of a parent's routine, it becomes a lesson in self-respect and self-preservation for children to absorb and emulate. These become patterns they will likely replicate in their own lives. What better lesson to teach our children, than to love themselves enough to spend time on themselves.

- **Demonstrating Balance:** By observing a parent's commitment to self-care, children learn the importance of balance. They come to understand life is not solely about obligations to others but also about honoring oneself.

- **Teaching Self-Value:** Children internalize the examples set by their parents. When they witness self-care in action, they learn valuing oneself is a natural and necessary part of life. This understanding is a gift that equips them to navigate the world with confidence and self-compassion.

- **Setting the Standard for Self-Care:** Parents who practice self-care set a standard for their children. They become the benchmark against which children measure their own worth and the care they and others deserve.

Self-care guides parents through the complexities of raising children. It gives us the power to go through our days with a more grounded sense of self and a heart full of compassion. It starts with you, but the care cascades to your children.

Now, we've learned that self-care is going to look different for everyone. Your routine should be tailored to fit your life, your values, and even sometimes your children. There are, however, a few things that are universal for all parents when we talk about self-care. Stress, sleep, and exercise are all things that should get a little bit of extra attention from you on your journey.

Stress Reduction

Stress has a way of overstaying its welcome. It arrives with the morning rush and lingers through the nighttime routine. Its presence is felt in every strained smile and furrowed brow. It can add to emotional overload and leave us feeling out of control, and out of touch with ourselves. Try these:

- **Morning Routine:** Consider starting each day with a ritual that signals a break from stress. A cup of tea in silence, a few pages of a beloved book—these simple acts are the first defensive strikes against the build-up of stress. Don't overthink this, it doesn't need to be planned and it doesn't need to be perfect. It just needs to feed your soul a little bit, it needs to ground you and give you some armor for the day.

- **Mindful Moments:** Integrate short, mindful practices throughout the day. Pause and take three deep breaths before answering a barrage of "whys" from a curious toddler, or step outside to feel the sun on your face for a brief respite.

These acts of self-care are not indulgent, they are necessary. You need to be stable, anchored, and unmanaged stress will slowly eat away at that.

Good sleep in a parent's life cannot be overstated. Adequate rest is a critical component of self-care, as it affects cognitive function, mood stability, and overall health. A good night's sleep can be elusive but prioritizing it can dramatically improve your ability to manage stress and anger.

CULTIVATING SLEEP HYGIENE

- **Consistent Schedule:** Aim to go to bed and wake up at the same time each day. This regularity trains your body's internal clock for more efficient rest. It goes without saying that we need to get the kiddos on board for this.

- **Sleep Environment:** Keep your bedroom dark, cool, and quiet. Consider blackout curtains, a fan, or white noise to create an optimal sleep setting.

- **Pre-Sleep Ritual:** Develop a calming pre-sleep ritual. This might include light reading, gentle stretching, or a warm bath to signal to your body it's time to rest. For an added bonus, these techniques can work on your children as well.

The benefits of regular exercise extend far beyond the physical. Exercise releases endorphins, the body's natural mood elevators. It can also be used to get rid of some of the emotional energy that might otherwise fuel anger. Whether it's a brisk walk in the fresh air, a dance session in the living room, or a structured workout, movement is a powerful tool for maintaining both physical health and emotional balance.

INCORPORATING EXERCISE INTO DAILY ROUTINES

- **Family Walks**: After dinner, take a walk together. It aids digestion and provides a space for casual conversation while engaging in moderate physical activity.

- **Playful Movement:** Turn household chores into an exercise routine. Squats while loading the dishwasher or calf raises while brushing teeth can be surprisingly effective. I personally like to incorporate dance parties into my clean-up routine with my children.

- **Exercise Snacking:** Scatter short bursts of activity throughout your day. Ten squats here, a 30-second plank there—it all adds up! It can also serve as a silly way to engage with your children.

These self-care practices can add a bit of resilience and vibrancy into your life. Stress relief leaves you feeling just a little bit lighter, regular exercise empowers your body, and adequate sleep restores your spirit so you can meet each day with renewed energy and perspective. Take special care to incorporate these as you rework your routines to fit your family, and to avoid potential triggers.

9

MAKING THE CHANGE: EMOTIONAL INTELLIGENCE

Imagine you are on the way home from picking your children up from school. You've had a bad day at work yourself, but you ask your children to tell you something good that happened to them today. Your daughter and son both excitedly start talking at once, and louder than you'd really like. You can't focus on them both, but you hear your daughter say that she got stickers at school for good behavior. You begin to tell her how proud you are that she is doing well in class, when your son yells "sissy!" and tries to hit her from his car seat. You look back to tell him that hitting is not okay, and that he is going to have a time out when you get home. You turn back around and wonder why you can just never have a peaceful day.

The answer might seem simple, but where does our emotional intelligence come into play here?

Emotional intelligence is our ability to gauge and understand our emotions, as well as the emotions of the people around us. Someone with a high emotional intelligence knows what triggers them, they understand what makes them happy, sad, jealous, and angry. They are also able to easily pick up on the state of other people's emotions. They can see when their spouse is feeling on edge, or when their child is being overstimulated. Using this sense of emotions allows them to react to situations differently than a person with a low emotional intelligence might.

There are a couple of different ways to use emotional intelligence in the scenario above. The first would be to understand that when we began this conversation with our children, we were probably already on edge. We know that our day at work didn't go well, and we left with shoulders strained from stress.

An emotionally intelligent parent would also be able to recognize why their son lashed out. At that moment, the child was really excited to share his day. When his sister began to talk over him, frustration probably settled in. Maybe he started talking just a little bit louder, hoping that the parent would be able to hear him over her. When the parent acknowledged what she said, in his eyes they were also ignoring him.

In that five second span of time, a child experiences a slew of different emotions. He was excited and happy, then frustrated and feeling unheard, and finally, angry. Was it okay for him to lash out physically or raise his voice? Of course not. The idea is that recognizing the root issue here could help you react in a way that could help avoid the same situation in the future. You want to be the parent that recognizes the emotions and acts accordingly.

Parenting, at its core, is an exercise in emotional intelligence. Parents are constantly managing the ebb and flow of feelings that move through our children. Sometimes they are calm and reflective, other times they might be wild and unpredictable. The depth of our understanding and our ability to guide them can shape not only their childhood but the adults they will become.

So, we know it's important, but how do we start being more emotionally intelligent?

Well, we start with recognition; we start by paying attention. We want to look beyond the reactive behaviors to the emotions that cause them. It's a change in the frame of our thinking that might feel unnatural at first but will eventually happen on its own. We want to see the child who pulls away from conversation at the dinner table and understand that they might just expect to be ignored. Maybe they aren't just bratty teenagers, maybe they feel like no matter how well they do, you aren't proud of them.

An important note here, it starts with you, so don't forget about yourself. Why do you react the way you do in certain situations? Do you disengage from play because you are worried about finances or because you are mentally still working? Do you react in anger to the dirty bedroom because you were punished as a child for a cluttered house? Being emotionally intelligent means being able to pick up on the little clues that we leave, and those that are children lead, to tell us where we are emotionally.

Here are some important notes and things to look for:

- Pay close attention to nonverbal cues, the language of the body often speaks louder than words. A downturned mouth, a furrowed brow, or a child avoiding your gaze can all be signals of a child's emotional state.

- Listen for the tone and pitch of their voice for the emotions at hand. Excitement reaches a higher pitch, while a child feeling sad may lower their tone. Understanding these subtle changes can offer insight into their feelings and allow you to act accordingly.

- Reserve judgment and approach each observation with a fresh perspective. Allow the child's current emotional state to stand on its own rather than be clouded by past behaviors.

How do we put it into practice, when we have that Eureka moment and see an opportunity with our child or with ourselves? Emotional outbursts, especially in younger children, are often the rawest expressions of their inner turmoil. Think of these moments as opportunities for connection and teaching, rather than for discipline. Responding with emotional intelligence can transform a potential conflict into a moment of growth for you, your child, and your relationship.

- Maintain a steady and calm presence. Your composure acts as a stabilizing force for your child when they feel anything but stable.

If they look up at you and your face is red in anger, or your fists are clenched in frustration, they are not going to feel safe.

- Validate their feelings, acknowledge that their emotions and concerns are legitimate and that they matter to you. This alone can be incredibly soothing, because it tells them that you see and accept their feelings, even if their behavior needs to change.

- Offer support without immediately trying to fix the situation. Sometimes the most potent response is simply to be there, offering a hug or a listening ear. It can be enough to just hold space and allow them to process their emotions in the safety of your presence.

When we respond to outbursts with emotional intelligence, we teach our children that their emotions are neither good nor bad—they simply are. This paves the way for the lesson that while we cannot choose our emotions, we have the power to choose our reaction to them.

Fostering an environment where emotions can be freely expressed requires patience. It involves making the space for feelings to unfold naturally, yet in a way that is healthy and constructive.

- Create regular opportunities for open dialogue when the day has settled, and your attention can be entirely focused on sharing and reflection. This is going to look different for every family, but no excuses. Maybe it looks like a five-minute conversation while you bathe your toddler, or everyone taking turns at the dinner table. You could dedicate a table in the house to judgment free listening. Creating a "listening" card to signal a need for emotional expression is also a great idea.

- Use storytelling and role-playing to explore emotions in a non-threatening way. Tales of characters experiencing fear, joy, or frustration can provide a safe distance from which to discuss these feelings. This will work better with younger children who won't find it annoying or juvenile.

- Celebrate emotional expression as a strength rather than a weakness. Applaud their courage in sharing their feelings and reinforce the message that emotions are a natural and valuable part of being human.

- This encouragement lays the groundwork for emotional intelligence. We want to instill in our children and ourselves the confidence to share our emotions, understand them, and manage them effectively.

We can use emotional intelligence to support ourselves, our children and help shape our lives so that self-awareness, resilience, and deep, meaningful connections thrive.

10

MAKING THE CHANGE: PAUSE

In the world of parenting, where the volume often feels turned up to high, the act of stepping into a quiet space can be revolutionary. Think of an adult time-out not as a retreat but as a strategic intermission. It's a chance to breathe, regroup, and return to your role as a parent with a refreshed perspective and calmer demeanor.

Imagine you're in the kitchen. Dinner's bubbling over, the dog's barking, and your child's rendition of a new song is on repeat. You recognize that you are feeling overwhelmed and overstimulated. Here, the power of a well-timed pause versus the desire to just get through it cannot be overstated. It's the deep breath before diving back into the pool of parenting duties, the quiet moment looking out the window, where you can regain perspective. Let's take a look at the difference it can make:

- **No pause**: You ignore the build up of tension in your body, because dinner needs to be made so that you can put the kids to bed and try to rest. You can't hear yourself think, let alone understand what your child says when you go to drain the pasta water. You are turning to the sink, and you run directly into the dog, and spill the boiling water. No one is hurt but you've had enough, and you yell at your child to be quiet and go away because they made you drop the pot.

- **Pause**: You recognize the signals that you are getting overwhelmed. You get down on your knees and tell your child that you need to take a time out, and they need to play in the other room. You stand by the stove, close your eyes, and breathe deeply. You focus on the smell of the sauce as you breathe, until you can feel your heartbeat slow down, and you start to feel less anxious. You finish up dinner, call your child, and sit down and enjoy your dinner feeling proud.

TAKE A TIME OUT!

A time-out is like hitting the reset button on a device when it's not functioning optimally. When emotions run high, and frustration clouds your thoughts, stepping away for a few minutes can offer a clear mind and a tempered heart. It can give you a quiet strength that is going to let you help restore harmony in the home.

But how do you know when to call for a time-out? If we could get away every time things got a little hectic around the house, we probably wouldn't be so angry in the first place. So, we need to be able to recognize the red flag, so we can raise the white one in the right moments. The signals might not always be loud and clear. Tuning into the subtler frequencies of your emotions and stress levels is key.

It's the tightening in your chest when toys are strewn across the floor again. The shortness of breath that accompanies another sibling squabble.

- **Watch for physical cues.** A clenching jaw, a knotted stomach, or a racing heart.

- **Notice emotional flags**. Irritation or impatience simmering just below the surface.

- **Be mindful of cognitive signals.** Scattered thoughts, difficulty concentrating, or waning attention.

Recognizing these things guides you to the realization a time-out is not just warranted, it's necessary. In these moments, you need to get to navigate away from the edge of emotional overflow and move towards tranquility. Get out of the danger zone.

COMMUNICATING YOUR NEED FOR A TIME-OUT TO YOUR CHILD

Honest conversations with your children about the necessity of personal time-outs helps to create an environment of mutual respect and understanding. It's about normalizing self-care and demonstrating its importance through your actions and words.

- **Age-Appropriate Explanation:** Share with your children, in words that they can understand, the idea of taking a moment to yourself to feel better.

Example:

Younger child: Mommy/Daddy's emotions are feeling really big, and I need a minute alone to calm them down.

Teenager: I'm feeling really overwhelmed, and I really need to take a moment.

- **Consistent Cues**: Establish a familiar signal that will tell them you need a pause. This can avoid conversations in a heated moment that might escalate, and it gives children a clear understanding of when you need these moments.

Example: You could use a "safe" word at home to ask for a pause. You could use the word pause, or even something silly like pineapple.

- **Involve Them in The Process**: Teach children their role during your time-out, whether it's engaging in a quiet activity or respecting a boundary.

Example: Walk your child to their bedroom when you need a time-out. Explain that it's their job to play quietly with a puzzle or toy until you are ready to come back and get them. An older child could listen to music or play on a computer.

- **Modeling Behavior**: Show your children that taking time-outs is a part of healthy emotional management, setting an example that they can emulate. Tell your child what the time-out does for you. Explain that you come back feeling relaxed and ready to try again.

Example: Before the time-out: Mommy/Daddy needs to take a time-out. I am feeling angry and I need to fix it.

After the time-out: Thank you so much for helping while I took a time-out. I had a snack, and wrote in my journal about my feelings while I was gone. I was feeling really upset before I left, but I wrote those feelings down, and now I feel much better.

In these open exchanges, children learn to recognize and respect not only their own need for space but that of others. It's a lesson that extends far beyond the home's walls.

GAIN SOME PERSPECTIVE

Sometimes, we're too close to something to be able to see the full picture. Similarly, when we're caught in the whirlwind of parenting, our perspective can become twisted. An adult time-out grants us distance so we can view the situation from a new angle. Whether it's understanding the root cause of a tantrum or recognizing a messy room isn't the end of the world, distance can bring clarity.

Perspective Shift Prompts:

- **Reflect on Intentions:** What are you hoping to achieve by responding to your child in this moment?

- **Consider Long-Term Impact**: How will your reaction influence your child's behavior and your relationship in the long run?

In the space of a time-out, grant yourself the freedom to observe your thoughts and feelings without critique or censure. You should be an unbiased observer, looking out and assessing the situation. Picture yourself as a gardener, looking over and assessing the well-being of your inner landscape.

- Acknowledge each emotion as it surfaces, whether it's a whisper of anxiety, a flutter of joy, or a shadow of frustration.

- Observe your thoughts without clinging to them or pushing them away.

- Consider your feelings and thoughts without attaching labels such as 'good' or 'bad'. They simply are, you are only acknowledging that they exist.

- If judgment arises, note it as well, and then return your attention to the role of observer. Be a witness to your own experience.

This practice of non-judgmental observation is a gentle tool to help you eliminate negative habitual reactions. It is an act of acceptance and lets us respond to life's conflicts with a more measured, compassionate approach.

RELIEVE STRESS

Stress accumulates in the body if we allow it to go unchecked. An adult time-out allows you to discharge this build-up before it is too late. Engaging in a calming activity, even for a short period of time, can significantly reduce stress levels.

The Emotional Reset Diagram

- Visualize Stress. Picture your stress as a color, filling your body.

- Imagine Release. With each breath during your time-out, visualize the color fading, representing your stress melting away.

Stress Relief Exercises

- **Five Senses Exercise:** Engage each of your senses to ground yourself. Find:

  o Five things you can see.

  o Four things you can hear.

  o Three things you can feel.

  o Two things you can smell.

  o One thing you can taste.

If that does not work for you, you could focus on each sense individually:

- **Touch:** Feel the fabric of your clothes against your skin, the air brushing against your cheek, or the firmness of the ground beneath your feet.

- **Sight:** Notice the interplay of light and shadow in your surroundings, the myriad of colors surrounding you, or the dust motes in a sunbeam.

- **Hearing:** Tune into the layers of sounds around you, from the distant chirping of birds to the hum of a refrigerator. Focus and identify each sound individually.

- **Smell:** Draw in the scents filling the air, whether the earthiness of rain-soaked soil or the aroma of freshly baked bread.

- **Taste:** Savor a sip of water, a piece of fruit, or a bit of chocolate, each flavor a unique sensation.

This immersion in sensory experience is a reminder the world is rich and varied, even in the most mundane moments—a truth easily forgotten in the hustle of parenting. It is a tool you can use to ground yourself and your body in the moment, while giving yourself an opportunity to relax.

Incorporating adult time-outs into your parenting approach isn't an admission of defeat. It's a strategic move towards better emotional management and healthier family interactions. Sensory awareness, and non-judgmental observation are not merely techniques. They are crucial for establishing a more mindful existence, both within the time-out and beyond it. They become our refuge, our respite, and our renewal.

BALANCING TIME-OUTS WITH PARENTAL RESPONSIBILITIES

Parenting is complex, the interplay between self-care and the ceaseless demand of child-rearing often requires a delicate balance. The concept of a quick time-out allows parents to maintain their composure without neglecting their duties. The key lies in establishing the seamless integration of these brief pauses into our routine in a way that will not serve as an interruption.

Quick Time-out Techniques

The luxury of extended solitude is rare for parents. Thus, swift and efficient time-out methods are needed. The methods we choose should be brief enough to insert between the acts of daily life, and strong enough to help us refocus and rejuvenate.

- **Sensory Reset:** Engaging a single sense intensely—a splash of cold water on the face, a burst of citrus scent—can act as a sensory cue to change your mental state.

- **Physical Anchors**: A series of shoulder shrugs or hand stretches can release physical tension, signaling to the mind a return to an at ease state.

- **Gratitude Flash**: Reflecting on a single point of gratitude can shift the mindset from stressed to thankfulness, it can provide a quick pivot that recalibrates emotional balance.

Example: I am thankful for having healthy, energetic children who are not afraid to share their emotions with me.

Involving Your Partner or Support Network

Parenting, though often a solo act, benefits from the support of a well-functioning family unit. Articulating the need for personal pauses to your partner or support system creates a shared understanding and a cooperative approach to managing family dynamics. In other words, ask for help, it really does take a village.

- **Syncing Schedules:** Aligning time-out periods with your partner's availability ensures that a parent is always present.

- **Tag Team:** Establish a system where one parent steps in when the other needs to step out, a fluid exchange that maintains harmony.

- **Backup Call**: When solo parenting, having a friend or family member on standby for quick relief can be invaluable.

- **Community Connection**: Engage with a network of fellow parents for mutual support, exchanging moments of respite as needed.

This network of support becomes a safety net, and it gives you an opportunity for reflection and relaxation when it is needed most. It also allows you to extend yourself grace without worrying that it will negatively impact your children.

11

MAKING THE CHANGE: BREATHE

You're standing at the kitchen counter, hustling to get breakfast served and the lunches packed. Your preschooler decides it's the perfect time to launch a full-scale protest against wearing socks. You can feel your heart begin to pace, and you sense your muscles tightening. So, you take a deep breath, and something shifts. The chaos doesn't disappear, yet you feel steadier, more anchored. That deep breath, as simple as it may seem, is a powerful tool you can choose to change the narrative.

Breathing is a natural pause button. It gives us the opportunity to gather our thoughts and center our emotions before responding, so breathe. It is a wall between you and the conflict that lets you get ready. It allows you to take control and guide the outcome.

OXYGEN AND BRAIN FUNCTION

Oxygen is the fuel that powers every cell. When we breathe deeply, we increase our bodies supply of oxygen, which can boost our cognitive abilities. The better we breathe, the better we think. You have a better chance at solving problems without letting negative emotions get the best of you.

Breath acts as a natural tranquilizer for the nervous system. Unlike stress responses which are hardwired into our brains and automatic, our breathing can be controlled with conscious effort. When we breathe deeply, we send a message to our brain to calm down and relax. The brain then forwards this message to our body. If we can't stop our bodies from freaking out, the next best thing is being able to tell them to cool it, and that is what breathing does.

By taking long, slow breaths, you can stop the tide of stress hormones preparing you to react and have a choice to respond calmly instead.

HEART RATE REGULATION

Our heart rate is closely tied to our emotional state. Anger can send the heart rate soaring, because it is preparing your body for action. We can guide our heart rate back to a steadier pace by slowing down our breathing. This can reduce feelings of stress and unease when we are in uncomfortable situations.

For instance, when your teen pushes boundaries, your heart rate may naturally rise. By focusing on your breath, you can keep the physical manifestations of anger at bay. This physical calmness can prevent the escalation of conflict, leading to a more thoughtful conversation about rules and freedom.

The power of breath in managing anger is a tool that doesn't require any special equipment or extensive training. It's accessible in the heat of the moment, and that makes mastering it invaluable.

SIMPLE BREATHING EXERCISES

Okay, so breathing is important, but when we are stressed and struggling it doesn't always come naturally. These age-old breathing practices are not complex, but their effects are profound. They allow us to approach each situation with a clear head and steady heart. Try a few and see which one works best for you.

Box Breathing

Imagine your breath moving around the four sides of a square. Each side represents a step in the breathing process — inhale, hold, exhale, hold. This visualization is at the heart of box breathing, a technique that can instill calm and focus.

- Begin by sitting upright in a comfortable chair, feet flat on the ground, hands resting gently on your lap.

- Close your eyes to eliminate distractions and focus entirely on your breathing.

- Slowly inhale through your nose while mentally counting to four, visualizing the first side of the square being drawn with your breath.

- Hold that breath for an equal count of four, completing the second side of the square in your mind.

- Gently exhale through your mouth for another count of four, tracing the third side of the square.

- Conclude the box by holding your breath once more for a final count of four, completing the square's last side.

- Repeat this pattern several times, allowing the rhythm to become second nature.

Parents can employ box breathing in those fleeting moments of downtime, after children are dropped off at school or in the stillness of a sleeping household. These techniques can also be taught to your children, which can help in moments where stress is running high for them.

Diaphragmatic Breathing

Diaphragmatic breathing, often referred to as "belly breathing," taps into the diaphragm's full range of motion, helping us to promote deep and efficient breaths. This type of breathing not only helps with managing stress but encourages proper oxygen exchange.

- Find a relaxed position lying on your back, maybe on a mat or a comfortable carpet, with your knees slightly bent and your head supported.

- Place one hand on your chest and the other on your abdomen, so that you can feel the rise and fall of each breath.

- Inhale slowly through your nose, directing the air downwards so your abdomen expands, like filling a balloon. The hand on your chest should remain relatively still.

- Exhale through slightly parted lips, engaging your abdominal muscles to empty the air completely. You will be able to feel the hand on your abdomen lower.

- Continue this breathing pattern, focusing on the sensation of your abdomen rising and falling. This movement encourages the diaphragm to contract and relax fully, activating the body's natural relaxation response.

This exercise can be easily done during nap times or those precious moments of quiet when the children are absorbed in play.

Lion's Breath

Drawing from yoga, Lion's Breath is an energizing practice that can help release tension and stimulate the mind. It's very useful for those moments when you need to reset your emotional state quickly.

- Choose a comfortable seated position, cross-legged on the floor or on a chair, with your spine straight and your hands resting on your knees.

- Inhale deeply through the nose, filling your lungs with air and gathering any tension or stress you've been holding onto.

- Open your mouth wide, stick your tongue out towards your chin, and exhale forcefully, making a "ha" sound. Imagine expelling all the pent-up energy with your breath.

- Relax your face and breathe normally for a few breaths before repeating the process two or three more times.

This exercise can assist you in releasing the day's emotional buildup. It's a technique that can be done in private or even made into a playful moment with children, teaching them a healthy way to express and manage their emotions.

Through practice, these exercises can become natural, a set of internal tools that parents can draw upon to maintain composure and presence.

INTEGRATING BREATHING TECHNIQUES INTO YOUR DAILY ROUTINE

Weaving moments of mindful breathing into daily life can transform the very quality of your being. We know they can help, but how do we actually include them in our day?

Morning Meditation

Morning meditation does not need to be a lengthy process; even a few minutes devoted to breathing can nourish the body and prepare the spirit for the day ahead.

- Wake up a few minutes earlier than everyone else. Find a comfortable spot, maybe a window where you can sit in the sunlight.

- Anchor yourself in the present with a series of deep, intentional breaths. Let the feeling of being able to begin a new day fill you with each breath.

- With each exhale, release any remnants of yesterday, allowing yourself to greet today with a heart unburdened by the past.

This morning meditation should become a protected time to connect with your inner self before responsibilities come calling.

Pre-Conflict Preparation

In families, disagreements and conflicts are natural. Anticipating these moments and preparing ourselves can change the way we navigate through them. Using breathing to prepare for conflicts can help you react to them in a way that isn't going to leave you feeling ashamed or guilty.

- Recognize the warning signs that typically come before a conflict, whether it's a particular time of day or a specific interaction.

- Pause and take a series of deep breaths, grounding yourself in the knowledge that you have the tools to manage the situation calmly.

- Visualize a positive outcome, using your breath to build a sense of inner peace that you can carry into the conversation.

- Approach the interaction with your breath serving as your support.

By incorporating these brief breathing exercises before entering a potentially heated exchange, you strengthen yourself against the rush of impulsive emotions. You can use them to ensure your words and actions are reflective of your true intentions.

Bedtime Relaxation

Integrating breathing techniques into bedtime routines can help both the parent and the child unwind and find rest. It also allows you to bond together in a positive setting.

- As you tuck your child in, share a few calm synchronized breaths together.

- Let your exhales be a lullaby, a soft and soothing rhythm that signals the body it's time to rest.

- In the stillness that follows, maintain the gentle pace of your breathing, allowing you to enter a state of relaxation.

- Carry this peace with you as you retire for the night, letting the day's challenges dissolve as you fall asleep.

This nightly practice not only aids in a more restful sleep but strengthens the bond with your child. Together you can find peace in the simple act of breathing.

When we add these practices into our daily routine, we create a space where calm prevails.

As we move through our lives, the practices we adopt become our current and future legacy. Intentional breathing is more than a strategy. It's a way of living, a gentle reminder that we have the capacity for tranquility and grace.

12

MAKING THE CHANGE: COMMUNICATE

Navigating the emotional terrain of parenting successfully, means having the right words at your disposal. You need to be able to identify, clarify, and communicate the full spectrum of feelings both you and your child experience. Having a verbal toolkit helps translate the most confusing of feelings into tangible terms that are easy for you and your child to identify.

DEFINING BASIC EMOTIONS

At the core of our emotional vocabulary are the basic emotions. While their meanings may come easily to you, oftentimes children struggle with them. They might not know exactly what they are feeling, and even if they do, it might be hard for them to put into words why they feel that way. When you arm yourself with these words, you make it easy for you to help your children develop emotional intelligence, and eventually emotional regulation.

- **Happiness.** An uplifted state that brings a sense of contentment and joy, it often manifests in smiles, laughter, and a general lightness of being.

- **Sadness.** This feeling is described as a sense of loss or disappointment, which may lead to tears, frowning, and isolating behaviors.

- **Fear.** It is an instinctual response to a perceived threat. Normally you would see a quickened heartbeat, a rush of adrenaline, and the urge to either protect oneself or flee. For many children, fear can manifest in an outburst of anger.

- **Disgust.** This is a reaction of revulsion or strong disapproval. It is most commonly related to unpleasant tastes, sights, or smells.

- **Anger.** Anger is an intense emotion stemming from frustration, injustice, or perceived harm, and it is usually accompanied by increased energy, irritability and sometimes aggressive behaviors.

- **Surprise.** Surprise is a brief state caused by an unexpected event, which can be either pleasant or unpleasant. A person typically shows a startle response when they are surprised.

By labeling these basic emotions, we give ourselves and our children a starting point for discussing our internal experiences. This process allows for emotions to be brought into the light, examined, and understood rather than being left in the shadows to fester.

EXPLORING COMPLEX EMOTIONS

As our emotional vocabulary expands, we begin to encounter more nuanced feelings. These are the complex emotions that arise from the blending of basic emotions.

- **Jealousy.** Often a mix of fear of loss and anger over perceived unfairness, jealousy requires careful navigation and open discussion to unravel.

- **Guilt.** Stemming from an inner conflict about actions or thoughts, guilt can be a catalyst for growth when addressed with compassion and reason. If guilt is left unattended, it can lead to issues with self-worth, and a person's ability to cope with conflict.

- **Pride.** This emotion combines happiness with a sense of accomplishment. Pride can boost self-esteem but requires balance to prevent it from tipping into arrogance.

- **Shame.** Unlike guilt, which relates to actions, shame touches on the self, it is a feeling of unworthiness. It takes care to unravel feelings of shame to restore a positive self-image.

- **Anticipation.** This is a forward-looking emotion that combines elements of fear, surprise, and interest; anticipation can motivate and inspire.

By exploring these complex emotions, we unlock a deeper level of emotional understanding with our children. This allows us to help them navigate their emotions and helps lead to their personal growth and emotional maturity.

EXPRESSING EMOTIONS IN HEALTHY WAYS

With a robust emotional vocabulary, the next step is to express these emotions in constructive ways. It's about finding the appropriate outlets and expressions to be sure that they contribute to our well-being and family harmony.

- **Use "I feel" Statements**: Start sentences with "I feel" rather than "You make me feel," taking ownership of your emotions and reducing the likelihood of defensive reactions from others.

Example: "I feel angry when someone comes into my private space", instead of "You make me angry when you come into my room".

- **Articulate the Cause**: When expressing emotions, be clear about what has triggered them. This helps others understand your perspective and can lead to more effective problem-solving.

Example: You interrupted me while I was on an important phone call. It's hard for me to think when two people are talking at once, and I feel angry when it happens.

- **Practice Active Listening**: When others express their emotions, listen intently and without interruption. This validation encourages emotions to be expressed more calmly and productively.

Example: Listen without thinking about what you are going to say next, or even about what happened before your child started speaking. Put yourself in their shoes, and listen to understand instead of reply.

- **Find Creative Outlets**: Encourage the expression of emotions through art, music, writing, or physical activity. These outlets can provide a safe space for emotions to be explored and understood.

Example: If your child is feeling angry, ask them to stop and do some push-ups or sit ups with you. You could even put on some music before you do so. Let them expel the emotions physically, and then communicate with them.

- **Teach Problem-Solving Skills:** Pair the expression of emotions with discussions about potential solutions or coping strategies, fostering resilience and a proactive mindset.

Example: "I hear that you are disappointed because your sister drew on your picture. What do you think we can do to fix it? It seems like your sister really wants to join you, maybe we can get her a page of her own, and you can remake your drawing."

By expressing emotions in a healthy manner, we model for our children how to navigate their inner world without being overwhelmed by it. We show them that emotions are powerful, but they are also manageable. We teach them that and expressing them is a sign of strength and self-awareness.

The emotional vocabulary we build and the way we choose to express them are vital components of our parenting toolkit. With every word we use to describe our feelings, we paint a picture of our emotional world for our children to see and understand. This becomes a map they can use to navigate their emotions and the emotions of those around them.

The right words at the right time can smooth the rough patches in our day. They can remind us of our strengths when we feel weak, offer patience when we're at our limit, and kindle understanding in the face of confusion.

Cognitive Restructuring

Cognitive restructuring is a process where you identify and challenge negative, often automatic, thought patterns, and replace them with more positive and realistic ones. When you notice yourself thinking, "I can't handle this," pause, and redirect. That's like a weed. Uproot it and plant, "I've handled tough situations before, and I can do this too."

Self-Perception Influence

The way we talk to ourselves shapes our self-perception. If our internal dialogue is harsh, we may view ourselves as inadequate parents. However, when we nurture our self-talk with kindness, our self-view shifts.

It's the end of a long day. You're trying to get dinner on the table and your kids are bickering over a toy. Your internal voice might chime in with, "Why can't I keep the peace?" Instead, try reframing it to, "I'm creating a home where my children feel safe to express themselves." This shift in self-talk alters your self-perception from a frazzled parent to a nurturing one.

Emotional Response Control

By controlling our self-talk, we can influence our emotional responses. We can begin to let ourselves make choices, instead of letting our emotions make them for us. We can take back the power. It's like holding the reins on a spirited horse—you're guiding the power, not letting it run wild. When a meltdown looms because your child won't wear their jacket on a chilly morning, reminding yourself, "I am the adult, I set the tone," can keep your emotions in check. It can help you respond with composure, rather than joining the meltdown.

CONSTRUCTIVE VS DESTRUCTIVE SELF-TALK

The thoughts that we allow ourselves to entertain internally either uplift us and offer encouragement or erode our confidence with criticism. Recognizing the difference between constructive and destructive self-talk is the first step in rewriting this internal narrative.

Negative Self-Talk Examples

- "I always mess up". A statement that leaves no room for the countless times you've succeeded or the fact everyone makes mistakes.

- "I should be better at this". This sets an unrealistic standard that doesn't account for the learning curve in parenting.

- "Why can't I have it together like other parents?". A comparison that discounts your unique circumstances and strengths.

- Each of these phrases closes the doors to growth and understanding. They leave us in a cycle of self-doubt and recrimination.

Positive Self-Talk Examples

- "I'm growing every day". This acknowledges parenting is a dynamic process and recognizes personal development.

- "Each challenge is a chance to learn". Here, the focus is on opportunity rather than fault, a perspective that fosters resilience.

- "I'm doing my best, and that's enough". A phrase that offers grace, reminding us that perfection is not the goal.

These expressions invite self-compassion and a recognition of our humanity. While they may feel silly to recite at first, they nudge us toward our potential.

In the ongoing self-talk narrative, there's a constant push and pull between the helpful and the unhelpful, the constructive and the destructive. The next time you catch yourself spiraling into a chorus of self-critique, pause and consider what you might say to a friend in the same situation. Chances are, you'd offer words of encouragement and support. Extend that same courtesy to yourself, and watch as the landscape of your parenting experience transforms before your eyes.

SELF-TALK TRANSFORMATION

Transforming self-talk from destructive to constructive is an active process that requires attention and patience.

- **Awareness**: Listen to the dialogue within yourself. When a negative phrase surfaces, pause and acknowledge its presence.

- **Challenge**: Confront these negative words. Question their validity, so often they're based on old fears rather than present realities.

- **Replace**: Craft a new dialogue that is rooted in positivity and truth. Select words that will build self-empowerment and kindness.

For instance, if the thought "I never do anything right" creeps in, stop it in its progression. Reflect on the moments you've succeeded, the times you've made your child laugh, and the nights you've soothed away nightmares. Replace it with "I have my successes and my challenges, just like everyone else."

- **Visualize**: Imagine yourself as the parent you aspire to be. How would this version of you talk to yourself? Let this image guide the way you speak to your children, and to yourself.

- **Practice**: Repeat these new, positive phrases regularly. They need time to become a natural response to challenges. They need time to take root in your mind and become the default setting.

As you begin to restructure the way you speak to yourself, keep these things in mind:

- **Start Small**: Don't attempt to overhaul your self-talk overnight. Start by focusing on one recurring negative thought. It is going to take time, so choose one that affects you the most negatively.

- **Write It Down**: Seeing the thought on paper can strip it of its power and make it easier to address.

- **Speak It Aloud**: Sometimes, hearing the negative thoughts spoken can highlight their harshness and absurdity. It can be really empowering to see just how judgmental our thoughts of ourselves really are.

- **Formulate a Positive Counterstatement**: Create a positive response that directly challenges the negative thought.

- **Repeat the Positive**: Use your new script, especially in moments when the old thought would typically arise. Repetition breeds familiarity.

This transformation is not about suppressing negative thoughts. It's about recognizing you can leave them in the past and choose a new path.

Your internal monologue is a constant companion. It can either lift you up or pull you down as you navigate the complexities of parenting. Deciding to alter the way you speak to yourself can transform the way you interact with your children. Engaging in constructive self-talk changes how you view yourself but also how you interact with and guide your children.

In the simplest terms, offer yourself the kindness you would want to see your children offer someone else.

CRAFTING YOUR POSITIVE AFFIRMATIONS

Personal Strengths Affirmations

Reflect on the instances when you have overcome challenges in your life. You can use them to build affirmations that are specific to you and struggles of everyday life. After all, this is about you. Use these reflections to build an army of affirmations that actually mean something to you.

- Acknowledge your resilience with affirmations like, "I have weathered many storms and emerged with wisdom."

- Celebrate your creativity. Perhaps it's the ingenious ways you handle a picky eater or the bedtime story that calms a restless mind affirming "My creativity enriches my family's life."

- Recognize room for growth by affirming, "Every experience enriches my parenting journey."

By focusing on these internal strengths, you reinforce the belief in your capabilities. It is very much a "speak it into existence" exercise.

Patience Affirmations

Patience is often perceived as a passive virtue. However, it is an active choice in the face of life's pressures. It's the deep breath we take before responding to a child's unending questions, the measured pause before addressing a spill. In creating affirmations around patience, you are preparing your mind for calm and thoughtful reactions.

- In moments of potential frustration, repeat, "I choose to respond with patience and composure."

- When time feels scarce, and the to-do list is large, affirm, "I give myself the gift of time, I understand that not everything needs to be rushed."

- As you face the learning curves of parenting, remind yourself, "I am patient with myself as I learn the best way to raise my child."

Love and Understanding Affirmations

The essence of parenting is love, and there is no doubt love is the reason you are here, looking for a way to change. Infusing your self-talk with affirmations of love and understanding can nurture you as a parent.

- In the daily interactions with your children, affirm, "My love is the compass that guides my actions and words."

- When misunderstandings arise, as they inevitably will, remind yourself, "I want to understand before being understood."

- To foster the bonds that unite your family, affirm, "My heart is open, and my love is unconditional."

These affirmations illuminate the path when the fog of frustration or fatigue sets in.

As you repeatedly practice these affirmations, you fortify the foundation upon which your family is built. One strong with patience, rich with understanding, and vibrant with the unyielding force of your love.

On a new day the mind, unburdened by the day's demands, can absorb the affirmations we offer it, planting seeds that will bloom throughout the hours ahead.

Morning Affirmations

Before the household wakes, you have an opportunity to set an intention for the day with affirmations that invigorate your spirit.

- As you awaken, greet the new day with a silent acknowledgment of its potential and your role within it.

- Affirm your ability to navigate the day with phrases like, "Today, I will find joy in the small moments with my children."

- Use these affirmations to anchor yourself in positivity. Let them be the first thoughts that guide your actions.

This practice allows a blend of foresight and hope, and it allows you to step into the day's rhythms with a proactive mind stance, ready to meet each challenge with a resilient spirit.

Conflict Resolution Affirmations

Conflict is not something that we are able to completely eliminate in our life. It is going to happen eventually, no matter how hard we try to avoid it.

It's in these instances that affirmations can serve as a counterbalance and help us to restore harmony.

- Remind yourself of your capacity for composure with affirmations like, "I maintain peace within myself even as I address conflict."

- Let these phrases guide you back to calm waters when disagreements arise.

- Embrace these affirmations as personal truths. Allow them to shape your approach to conflict with empathy and clarity.

With these words echoing in your thoughts, you're better equipped to engage in discussions that end in resolution. You are fostering an environment where every family member feels heard and valued.

Evening Reflection Affirmations

As dusk settles and the pace slows, it's a time to honor the day's efforts and release any lingering tensions.

- Close the day with affirmations that acknowledge your endeavors and the love that fueled them, such as, "I gave my best to my family today, and that is enough."

- Let these affirmations be a gentle closing for any lingering negative thoughts about your actions or interactions throughout the day.

- Through these nightly affirmations, grant yourself permission to rest, knowing that you actively made choices today to improve. You have poured your heart into yourself, your children and parenting.

This nightly practice wraps the day in a soft embrace, allowing you to let go of any imperfections and focus on the love and dedication that defined your day. Concentrating on your strength, self-compassion, and commitment to your family can help to avoid falling into negative thoughts like, "I could have done more". In the quiet that ends the hustle of daily life, these affirmations are whispers of strength, self-compassion, and unwavering commitment to your family.

With each day's rise and fall, remember the power that resides in your affirming words. The power to uplift, guide, and soothe. They are the soft-spoken heroes of your narrative, the quiet architects of a family life built on understanding, patience, and the power of positive thought.

Reflective Self-Talk Worksheet:

- List common negative self-talk phrases you use.

- Reflect on the impact these phrases have on your mood and actions.

- Rewrite these phrases into positive affirmations.

- Practice using these affirmations daily, especially during challenging parenting moments.

Self-Talk Awareness Quiz:

- Rate the frequency of negative vs. positive self-talk you engage in during parenting challenges.

- Identify triggers that prompt negative self-talk.

- Commit to a plan for increasing positive self-talk when triggers occur.

By understanding and reshaping our internal dialogue, we're not just changing words; we're changing our parenting reality.

13

MAKING THE CHANGE: BOUNDARIES

B oundaries within a family create the structure needed for each member to flourish. They are the invisible fences that protect. The guidelines that empower. The clarity that nurtures growth and respect. They are sometimes also the only things that keep us from absolutely losing it on our children.

Setting boundaries is less about imposing rules and more about sculpting the space in which freedom and responsibility can coexist.

THE IMPORTANCE OF BOUNDARIES IN PARENTING

Boundaries in parenting provide the necessary signals that help maintain flow, ensure safety, and allow everyone to reach their destinations without unnecessary collisions. In other words, boundaries are what allow everyone in your home to exist, as themselves, without making it hard for someone else to exist.

Fostering Mutual Respect

When parents establish clear boundaries, they send a message of respect to their children, acknowledging their growing need for personal space and autonomy. In turn, children learn to respect these boundaries, understanding them as necessary within the family dynamic. For instance, a parent might establish a boundary around their home office, explaining that during certain hours, it's a space for work. This not only ensures the parent can focus but also teaches the child to respect others' needs for uninterrupted time.

Encouraging Independence

Boundaries are not just barriers. They are teaching your child how to be independent. By setting boundaries around certain behaviors or responsibilities, parents encourage children to make choices within a safe framework. For example, a set bedtime for a school-aged child establishes a clear expectation while also allowing the child to develop a routine and make decisions about how to spend their evening time before lights out.

Enhancing Communication

Clear boundaries enhance transparency in communication by setting out clear expectations and consequences. Consider the family mealtime. A boundary might be devices are turned off so the family can engage with each other. This communicates the value placed on face-to-face interaction and allows everyone to be mentally present, strengthening family ties.

Boundary Setting Exercise:

- **Identify**: What boundaries do you feel are currently lacking in your family? Is it uninterrupted sleep, respect for privacy, or adherence to house rules? Are there any recurring triggers for you, or even your child that could be addressed with a boundary?

- **Discuss**: Have a family meeting to talk about these boundaries. Why are they important? How do they benefit everyone? Engage your children here, give them an opportunity to express a boundary that might make a difference to their mental health.

- **Implement**: Put the agreed-upon boundaries into practice. Use visual reminders, like a chart on the fridge, if needed. Consistency is so important here. If there is no change, there will be no follow through.

- **Reflect**: After a week, reflect on how these boundaries have changed the family dynamic. What's working? What needs tweaking?

Real-life Boundary Scenarios:

- **Scenario 1**. Your teenager asks to go to a late movie on a school night. The boundary is clear—school nights are for rest. However, you can discuss the reasons behind this boundary to reinforce its importance and show it's in place out of care for their well-being. Remember, boundaries are about coexisting harmoniously, if there is a compromise, suggest it.

- **Scenario 2**. Your eight-year-old wants to play in their room alone. You respect their need for personal space (a boundary you've established) but also set a time limit, after which they will join the family for dinner, fostering a balance between independence and family time.

- **Scenario 3**. Your preschooler is learning about personal boundaries. Use simple language to explain why we knock on doors before entering or why we don't interrupt when someone is speaking. These are boundaries that teach respect and patience.

By setting boundaries that foster mutual respect, encourage independence, and enhance communication, you are setting your family up for a more peaceful home.

In the spaces where boundaries are respected, trust grows. It may seem slow to stick, but just wait for the moment when a child waits patiently while their sibling finishes speaking. It's in the shared glances that say, "I see you, I hear you, I honor the space you need." Boundaries, in their essence, are the silent affirmations of a family's love and respect for one another.

TECHNIQUES FOR SETTING BOUNDARIES WITH YOUR CHILD

Okay, so we know that boundaries are important, we know they can make a difference, but how do we set them? Each instance of boundary setting guides behavior and shapes character. It is going to take a lot of intention, and even more attention. The trick is making the boundaries and communicating them in a way that your child can understand. We need to make them supportive to the household but not restrictive. Clear but not constricting. It's a delicate balance, and it will take time and consistency to get it right.

Clear and Concise Language

Children love to find a good loophole, so when you are setting boundaries, don't leave room for interpretation.

- Use direct statements that outline the expectation and the reason behind it. If bedtime is set at 8 PM, explain that clearly: "Bedtime is at 8 PM because rest is important for your health and happiness."

- Avoid complex phrases or idioms that might confuse your child. It is seriously unlikely that they will stop you to gain understanding. Children benefit from straightforward communication that makes the rules and their purpose clear.

- When setting a boundary, ensure the language matches the child's cognitive level. For younger children, simple phrases work best: "We use gentle hands with our friends."

Engaging children in boundary discussions can also aid in clarity. Ask them to repeat back the boundaries in their own words. This not only confirms their understanding but also reinforces the rule through their active participation. This is especially important when a boundary is broken, and it probably will be at one point or another.

Consistent Enforcement

Every single one of them would argue it, but children need rules. Boundaries are the framework for a child to learn to navigate the world, and consistency is key. When parents enforce boundaries reliably, children understand the predictability of outcomes, which in turn fosters a sense of security and trust.

- Maintain uniformity in how rules are applied. If screen time is limited to one hour, this limit should be upheld consistently, not sporadically. The more you deviate, the more they will deviate.

- Caregivers should be aligned in boundary enforcement. Mixed messages can lead to confusion and manipulation as children learn to navigate adult inconsistencies. Communicating with your spouse, co-parent, and babysitters is essential.

- When a boundary is crossed, respond with predetermined and discussed consequences. This teaches children actions have consistent and understandable results. A boundary is there so everyone can expect how things will happen in the home; it should be the same for the consequence.

In moments when boundaries must be flexed—such as a special occasion or an emergency—communicate this to the child as an exception to the rule, not a new rule. This is another opportunity to have the child repeat back the boundary, and that they understand that this is an exception. The boundary needs to be maintained.

Age-Appropriate Boundaries

As children grow, their worlds expand, and with this expansion should come the evolution of boundaries. What is appropriate for a toddler will not be for a teenager. Our boundaries need to change as our children change.

- For young children, boundaries often revolve around safety and basic behavior—no touching the stove, no hitting siblings. These are the first steps in understanding the concept of limits.

- School-aged children can handle more complex boundaries—completing homework before screen time, for example. These boundaries begin to intertwine with personal responsibility and self-discipline.

- Teenagers who are exploring independence require boundaries that respect their growing autonomy while still providing guidance—curfews that are reasonable, privacy that is honored, expectations that are tied to their ability to self-regulate.

The key is communication and inclusion, where children of all ages are involved in the boundary-setting process. This not only ensures the boundaries are age-appropriate but also gives children a sense of ownership over the rules they are expected to follow.

Boundaries are going to help your child develop their own sense of self. They are able to do this while also getting a basic knowledge of how the world works outside of the home. You need to find a delicate balance between guidance and freedom.

COMMUNICATING YOUR BOUNDARIES EFFECTIVELY

Setting boundaries allows everyone to participate more confidently because they know what's expected. Establishing these guidelines is only half the task. Expressing them in a way that fosters understanding and acceptance is where the true craft lies. In other words, the boundary is nothing if no one understands it. The methods we choose to communicate boundaries can make all the difference. So how exactly do we set the boundary effectively?

Non-Violent Communication

Within the family dynamic, the method of non-violent communication (NVC) serves as a gentle but powerful means of expressing boundaries. This approach uses empathy and clear, empathetic language, avoiding any form of emotional harm.

- **Begin with observation, free of evaluation:** Describe the behavior that's challenging without attaching judgment.

Example: You are playing really roughly with me.

- Express emotion without blame. Share how the behavior affects you using "I feel" statements.

Example: I feel upset and a bit angry when I am being hit.

- Clarify needs. Explain what needs of yours are connected to the emotions you're experiencing.

Example: I need to feel safe and loved and I don't feel like that when you play roughly.

- Make requests, not demands. Ask for specific actions that would meet your needs while being open to dialogue.

Example: Please stop hitting me and find another way to play with me. If you need to get energy out, we can find another way to do that. Do you have any ideas?

This method pivots on respect for the child's feelings and perspectives, ensuring the boundary is seen not as a decree but as a natural extension of family cooperation. Your child should feel like you are solving a problem together, instead of feeling like they are the problem.

Active Listening

When parents actively listen to their children's responses to boundaries, they do more than hear words. They signal a willingness to engage in a two-way conversation. It lets your child know that you hear them, but you also see them. You understand and value their feelings, perspectives, and needs.

- Offer your full attention when your child reacts to a boundary. This can diffuse defensiveness, showing that their perspective matters.

Example: You: No, you cannot stay out late tonight. It is a school night, and you need rest.

Teenager: It's not fair, you never let me stay out. My friends are all allowed, and I know when I am tired.

- Reflect back on what has been said to ensure understanding. This can help clarify the boundaries and address any misconceptions.

Example: You: You want to stay out with your friends and have fun, that's totally understandable. You feel like I never let you do that, and I can totally see how that could be frustrating.

- Invite your child to offer their thoughts on the boundary, validating their feelings while maintaining the importance of the rule.

Example: You: It's understandable to feel frustrated and even a little angry at me. It sucks when you feel like you are being treated unfairly. We set this boundary because you are important, and your body deserves rest. We can talk about it more if you want and see if we can come up with a day or activity for you and your friends to do.

Through this responsive dialogue, boundaries are established in family life with mutual respect and shared understanding.

POSITIVE REINFORCEMENT

Focusing on the positives when setting boundaries can be really powerful. Positive reinforcement celebrates the actions that align with family expectations, reinforcing the behavior you want to see more often. Think about the times when you react to a behavior by yelling, your child may continue the behavior because you reinforced it with attention. Try to acknowledge the behaviors you want and redirect the ones you don't.

- **Acknowledge when your child respects a boundary.** This positive feedback encourages them to continue observing the rule.

Example: Wow buddy, good job knocking and waiting for daddy to come out of the bathroom.

- **Use rewards judiciously to reinforce adherence to boundaries.** These should not be bribes but acknowledgments of good behavior.

Example: Since you waited so nicely for me, do you want to go outside and play for a bit?

- **Share successes**. When boundaries lead to positive outcomes, highlight these moments as victories for the whole family.

Example: (At the dinner table) You: Johnny was so patient today. He even waited outside of the bathroom for me instead of just walking in.

Through positive reinforcement, children learn respecting boundaries is not only appreciated but is also rewarding in its own right. Most children have a deep seeded desire to make you proud. Make sure to notice the moments when they take what you say and try their best to not only listen but act.

 Communicating boundaries is a process that unfolds in everyday moments. Those small, meaningful exchanges where boundaries are shared and understood help the family to thrive.

BOUNDARIES AS A TOOL FOR ANGER MANAGEMENT

Emotion and control are intricately connected. Boundaries serve as guardians of control against the surge of overwhelming emotion that can lead to anger, channeling the flow of daily stresses into manageable streams.

Preventing Overwhelm

Within the family, each member carries their own load of life's demands. Without boundaries, the weight can become too much, inviting in frustration and anger. Boundaries act as a support for each person, creating clear limits to prevent the piling up of too many expectations or responsibilities. Think about how much weight could be taken off of your shoulders, if your kids just picked up their clothes off of the floor or cleared their own dinner plates.

- Assign roles and responsibilities that align with each family member's capacity. Acknowledge everyone has a threshold that, when respected, maintains balance.

Explain it in terms they can understand. If your child is young, a visual might even help. Have your child stack a pile of books in your arms and tell them that they are the chores around the house. Have them add a book for each additional chore, so they can see how not helping can be really hurtful.

- Create routines that include downtime, ensuring space for relaxation and recharge-as vital as the air we breathe.

- Emphasize the value of saying no or not now, teaching children it's acceptable to set their own limits in the interest of self-preservation. This can also give you the confidence of knowing that your children are able to hold their ground and say no when it is needed outside of the home.

Reducing Conflict

We know we aren't going to be able to completely eliminate conflict. It's just not a realistic goal for anyone. We can use boundaries to reduce the amount of conflict in the house.

- It's hard for any group of people to be together all the time. Personalities clash, just like our wants and needs do. Establish a time where everyone can feel able to speak freely about any boundary concerns.

- Establish zones within the home where tranquility is the rule, such as a reading nook or a listening corner, providing havens for calm amidst the hustle of family life.

- Agree on shared values that act as the family's compass, guiding actions and reactions, and serving as common ground from which resolutions can arise.

Encouraging Self-Control

The capacity for self-control is like a muscle that strengthens with use. Boundaries are the weights that provide the resistance needed for growth. For children especially, understanding the limits of behavior and the consequences of stepping beyond them is a foundational lesson in self-regulation.

- Instill decision-making opportunities within safe parameters, allowing children to experience the outcomes of their choices. This reinforces the concept of self-control. They need to feel the negative consequence of making a bad decision as much as they need the reinforcements of good decisions.

- Celebrate moments when self-restraint is successfully exercised. Providing positive reinforcement encourages the continued development of this crucial skill. This goes for you too Momma/Daddy.

- Model self-control through your own adherence to boundaries, demonstrating restraint is not a limitation but a form of self-respect and respect for others. Show your children, as well as telling them.

As self-control around boundaries grows so too does the ability to navigate emotions without being overwhelmed. Almost everything we've talked about centers around raising your awareness of yourself. Everything stems from that.

We carry with us the lessons learned in the spaces between our boundaries. It is here we find the true essence of family—love, respect, and mutual regard.

14

EMERGENCY STASH

It can be really difficult to train your mind to respond differently to the anger we experience daily as parents. You aren't always going to have time to re-read a chapter to give you some direction in your times of need. Remembering the 3 R's of anger management, or even just giving them a quick skim, can make a huge difference on your journey.

THE 3 R'S: RECOGNIZE, REFLECT, AND RESPOND

The 3 R's of anger management include recognize, reflect, and respond. Think of them as a rolled-up version of this book. If you find yourself in a position of anger, and thinking through the haze of your emotions is hard, they can come in handy. They walk us through, from start to finish, how to navigate the situation calmly.

- **Recognize**: Look for the emotion and look for the distress signals from your body and mind. Are you feeling like you just want to get away, like you need to lash out, or are you feeling sad. Maybe your heart is starting to race, or you are beginning to feel shaky. Maybe you can feel the tension beginning to mount in your hands or jaw. Recognize these things for what they are, anger rising just below the surface.

- **Reflect**: Take a moment to reflect on what is happening and give yourself some self-care. Pause, take an adult time out, or utilize a breathing technique. Use the time to tune into yourself and your emotions. Gain some understanding and identify the trigger. Knowing what is wrong, is going to help you take the next step. Don't reinsert yourself until you have been able to separate yourself from the anger and are confident that your response will encourage a positive outcome.

- **Respond**: Utilize the techniques we have learned through the book to tailor your response to the situation. Use your emotional intelligence to change perspectives and communicate your needs effectively. Maybe you need to set a boundary, do so with a firm but non-argumentative tone.

This method of thinking can be used in any situation where you feel like an emotional outburst might be impending. It's an easy, reliable way to guide you to a controlled, compassionate response.

You can also use this list of common issues and solutions to give you inspiration when things are beginning to get rocky. Even if they are not the exact situation you are experiencing, they can remind you of the actions you can take to encourage a positive outcome.

Common Parenting Triggers and practical solutions:

- **My child is not listening:** Choose a signal that your child can use to show you they are actively listening. Personally, I have my children put their "listening ears" on. You could have them touch their nose, sit on their hands, or even go to a specific place in the house. They should understand that when you say listening ears/touch your nose, everything stops and their attention needs to be on you. Wait until they have given you the signal to continue. It won't matter how many times you say something if your child is not in the mind space to give you attention. This combines a pause and communicating your need for active listening.

- **My child is whining:** Tell your child that you cannot understand them when they talk like that, and act like you really can't understand. It may take a few tries for them to get the point, but when they realize they will not get through to you, they will try another way. You are reinforcing communication skills.

- **Sibling Arguments:** Your first step is going to be to separate them, so that you all have a moment to pause, and breathe. If they are not able to communicate verbally after that, you could have each of them sit and write a letter from the other person's point of view. This gives you some quiet time and your children some time for reflection/empathy. They can exchange them when they are calm and ready to speak and listen respectfully. The idea here is not about blame, but managing your stress level, and encouraging communication, and mutual respect.

- **My child won't stop crying:** Give your child a drink of water (it's really hard to drink and cry) and invite them to take some deep breaths with you. Place their hand on their chest and ask them to pay attention to how it moves. Try to keep their attention on either your mouth, or their hand. Count the breaths as you go. Another method would be to ask them to smell the flower and blow out the candle. Communicate that you cannot help them, if you can't understand them. If all else fails, and you feel yourself getting ready to blow, separate yourself, and come back.

- **My child doesn't respect my space:** Set the boundary with your child and ask them to mirror it back to you. Depending on age, it might even help to get some colored electrical tape to clearly set the physical boundary for your child. Explain the consequence of crossing the boundary and follow through. This may take a few tries, but if you are consistent, the behavior will decrease or stop.

ASK FOR HELP

Don't do this alone. ask for help. I know that this is something that you've probably heard a thousand times, but that is because it is important. You need a support system behind you to fall back on. This is going to look different for everyone, but it is vital, nonetheless.

- **Spouse / Partner**: If you are working on managing your life without anger, it is something that your spouse needs to be aware of and on board with. Maybe you have a spouse that operates differently than you and doesn't struggle with anger. Their role might be to hold you accountable or remind you of techniques you can use when you are feeling emotional. It's possible your spouse struggles with anger too and needs to begin to make changes for the sake of your children. Communicate with them, make them understand your desire to live differently, and encourage them to do the same.

- **Family**: This can include your immediate family, as well as those that live outside of the home. Tell your children what you are trying to do, be transparent about what you've learned about yourself, and the changes you want to make. Chances are that a happier more peaceful home is something they will want to see as well. Use your extended family to help you on your journey if you can. Ask them for help in the moments where you know that five minutes of self-care is just not going to do it. Ask them to enforce boundaries and encourage positive communication when your children are with them.

- **Friends**: Your friends can play a huge part in helping manage your anger. It can be intimidating to open up about struggles with control, but the right friends are going to want to act as a support system. They might be able to offer advice that worked for them in their own struggles. They might offer to help with the kids so that you have some time to get in tune with yourself, and just feel like a person again. Even if they aren't able to do any of that, they can serve as an ear when you just feel like you need to be heard.

- **Community**: Reach out, there are parents out there struggling just like you are. Find people who share the same experiences as you and exchange support. You can talk war-stories and strategies, or just simply revel in the fact that you are not alone.

15

TAILORING YOUR ANGER
MANAGEMENT BLUEPRINT

You've gone through a lot in the last couple of chapters. You've learned a ton of new information, gained a lot of insight, and confronted some deep, and likely challenging issues. You have a list of strategies to use in your journey towards anger management. It's a lot to take in, and no one would blame you if you still felt a little lost about how to get started.

Luckily, there is a worksheet to help you put everything we've gone through into action. It's going to help you create a realistic plan that is tailored to you, your needs, and your values.

It is going to be the start for you but remember that consistency is important. Use this exercise as you grow on your journey. As you make progress, and as new challenges present themselves, create a new version for yourself. Not only will this mindset help you lay the foundation for change, and root you in a new mindset, it will allow you to see how much progress you have made!

WORKSHEET

A. Identify Triggers

Make a list of your most common anger triggers. Include the times they occur and any underlying issues. For instance, "My toddler refuses to get dressed in the morning and I'm worried I'll be late for work and my boss will be mad at me".

Trigger 1:

Trigger 2:

Trigger 3:

B. Choose Coping Strategies

For each trigger, select one to two coping strategies from among those you've learned from this book, such as deep breathing, mindfulness, positive affirmations, and self-care. Be specific, and make sure that the strategies you have chosen make sense. If your trigger is your child won't leave the playground without throwing a fit, reading a book for five minutes is probably not going to help.

Strategy Trigger 1:

Strategy Trigger 2:

Strategy Trigger 3:

C. Set Short-Term Goals

Create a few immediate and attainable objectives to let you know you're building the foundation for more significant change, like "I will speak quietly when I feel like yelling, or even I will apologize after not communicating calmly and compassionately."

Short-Term Goal 1:

Short-Term Goal 2:

Short-Term Goal 3:

D. Long-Term Goals

Set goals for where you want to be in a few months in your parenting journey, such as 'Within 3 months, I will firmly establish the habit of using active listening with my child". Make the goals measurable, and attainable.

Long-Term Goal 1:

Long-Term Goal 2:

Long-Term Goal 3:

Once you feel like you've mastered a trigger, or you've reached a goal, swap the paper out. There is always work to be done, but the more you work at it, the sweeter it will become. You'll find yourself rewarded with a child who feels like they can share with you, or the serenity of a space in your house where people respect your privacy.

CONCLUSION

Anger is an unfortunate part of all of our lives. It can rob us of so many things if it is left unmanaged. You can find yourself without control, in a place that doesn't even feel like home anymore. It can alienate your relationships with your children, friends and co-workers. It can leave you feeling unhinged, and behaving in ways that directly contradict your values, morals, and desires in life.

It can be scary to find yourself knee deep in an anger that you don't understand, but we've learned throughout this book that you can learn to understand it. You can identify where it comes from, and why it decides to choose to invade your life in the moments that it does. We've discovered our personal triggers, how unresolved past traumas can haunt us, and how our life outside of home can contribute to emotional overload. We've learned to take a deeper look at ourselves and our children, and how we affect each other. Most importantly, we've learned a few ways we can get ahead of the anger, before it consumes us.

You are about to close the page on this book, and hopefully start a new chapter of your life. It sounds cliche, but that is the idea behind this book, and the silent hope that you had when you picked it up. The hope is that you leave, with a renewed sense of control, ready for a new beginning. You were brought here by the desire to create a picture of balance, love, and understanding for your home. You stayed because you wanted to see that become a reality for you and your children.

Throughout this book, we've laid out strategies, techniques, and heartfelt guidance, each piece carefully chosen to support you, teach you, and help you realize that your anger doesn't have to own you. It has to play a role in your life, and everyone else's, because that is how we are built, but you are the main character. You can take control, make the choice, and make the change.

A few things before you go:

The Role of Consistency in Anger Management

Your commitment to consistency is going to make the difference. It's what take's the ideas and makes them transformative habits. You might not see the progress at first, and it is probably going to take longer than you like, but if you stick with it, it will happen. Choose a strategy and choose consistency. Implement them with a promise to yourself, because you deserve a life with less anger, and more joy, love, and harmony.

Recognizing and Celebrating Your Progress

DO NOT forget to celebrate, especially the little things. Each time you choose patience over frustration, or respond with empathy rather than anger, you lay another stone and build a stronger foundation for yourself and your family. Celebrate and share these victories, both big and small. Let them become motivations to keep pushing and to make bigger goals.

Your Crucial Role in Creating a Harmonious Family

Never underestimate the power of your influence in your family. You are important, you are valued, you are loved. As a parent, you very literally create your child's world, make it a beautiful one. Give them resilience, empathy, and emotional intelligence and watch what they build within the space you create for them.

A Final Word of Encouragement and Hope

It's not easy, looking anger in the face and knowing that it has made you into someone you don't recognize, even if it's just for a moment. It's not easy to admit that you are not in control, and you need help. You made it here though, because you love your family and hopefully because you love yourself. This isn't going to be easy either, and you are going to falter, but you won't fail.

Your family will see your resilience, strength and patience and want to rise up to meet you. It's not going to happen overnight but when it does, I hope you feel surrounded by the same love, support, and compassion that you've worked to give to your family.

Share the Torch: Your Review Ignites Change

Having mastered the art of managing emotions, transforming communication, and creating a nurturing environment in your home, it's now your turn to illuminate the path for others.

By sharing your honest review of this book on Amazon, you do more than express your viewpoint; you guide other parents to the resources they've been searching for. Your insights can fuel their journey towards a more harmonious family life, passing on the flame of knowledge and understanding about effective anger management.

We extend our heartfelt thanks for your contribution. The movement towards better parenting through anger management thrives on the exchange of wisdom — and by sharing your experience, you play a crucial role in this continuous cycle.

Zap the QR code right here to share your thoughts:

In this shared quest for peaceful parenting, your review is a powerful gesture of support to families navigating similar challenges. It's not just about helping others find this book; it's about affirming that they are not alone in their struggles and that transformation is within reach.

Thank you for choosing to pass on your newfound knowledge. Your voice is instrumental in spreading hope, inspiring change, and fostering a community of parents dedicated to raising confident, content children in a peaceful home. Together, we keep the spirit of positive change alive and well.

Also, if you would like complimentary extras, please visit our website at www.nonfictionnucleus.com.

REFERENCES

A systematic review of neural, cognitive, and clinical ...
https://www.ncbi.nlm.nih.gov/pmc/articles/PMC9174026/

Controlling your anger as a parent
https://www.pregnancybirthbaby.org.au/controlling-your-anger-as-a-parent

3 Ways to Be Emotionally Detached https://www.wikihow.com/Be-Emotionally-Detached

How Anger Rules Over Some Families
https://www.psychologytoday.com/us/blog/between-the-generations/202208/how-anger-rules-over-some-families

Parenting stress: What causes it, and how does it change us?
https://parentingscience.com/parenting-stress/

Parenting under pressure: Impact of Work-Life balance on ...
https://www.linkedin.com/pulse/parenting-under-pressure-impact-work-life-balance-chandra-sekhar-l

Recurring Parent-Child Conflict: A Mediator between ...
https://www.ncbi.nlm.nih.gov/pmc/articles/PMC9635455/

Stress Management for Parents - Child Development Institute
https://childdevelopmentinfo.com/how-to-be-a-parent/angry_child/stress/

Anger and Trauma - National Center for PTSD
https://www.ptsd.va.gov/understand/related/anger.asp

The Science of Generational Patterns: From Trauma to ...
https://www.jaiinstituteforparenting.com/the-science-of-generational-trauma

Healing Guilt: 7 Steps to Self-Forgiveness
https://www.psychologytoday.com/ca/blog/mindful-anger/202006/healing-guilt-7-steps-self-forgiveness

12 Examples of SMART Goals for Anger Management
https://successindepth.com/smart-goals-for-anger-management/

The Importance of Oxygen for Brain Health and Cognitive ...
https://www.boostoxygen.com/the-importance-of-oxygen-for-brain-health-and-cognitive-function/

Breath control helps quell errant stress response
https://www.health.harvard.edu/mind-and-mood/relaxation-techniques-breath-control-helps-quell-errant-stress-response

3 Breathing Techniques for Anger Management
https://boardwalkrecoverycenter.com/3-breathing-techniques/

Top 5 Breathing Exercises to Practice Daily (And the Best ...
https://resbiotic.com/a/blog/top-5-breathing-exercises-to-practice-daily-and-the-best-times-to-do-them

Self-talk - what is it and why is it important?
https://www.healthdirect.gov.au/self-talk

[Parental involvement in cognitive-behavioral therapy for ...
https://pubmed.ncbi.nlm.nih.gov/25219692/

The Psychology of Self-Talk: A Deeper Look into Our Inner ...
https://www.linkedin.com/pulse/psychology-self-talk-deeper-look-our-inner-john-r-kormanik-esq-

Positive Thought Affirmations for Managing your Anger
https://affordablequalitycounseling.com/positive-thought-affirmations-for-managing-your-anger/

Could Mindfulness Help You Control Your Anger?
https://greatergood.berkeley.edu/article/item/could_mindfulness_help_you_control_your_anger

Stress Management for Parents - Child Development Institute
https://childdevelopmentinfo.com/how-to-be-a-parent/angry_child/stress/

Effective Communication with Children: Nurtifying Strong ...
https://quenza.com/blog/knowledge-base/effective-communication-with-children/

Effectiveness of Parent-to-Parent Support Group in ...
https://www.ncbi.nlm.nih.gov/pmc/articles/PMC9615447/

Parenting stress: What causes it, and how does it change us?
https://parentingscience.com/parenting-stress/

Strategies for controlling your anger: Keeping anger in check
https://www.apa.org/topics/anger/strategies-controlling

How to Cope With Emotions Using Distraction - PTSD
https://www.verywellmind.com/coping-with-emotions-with-distraction-2797606

Strategies for controlling your anger: Keeping anger in check
https://www.apa.org/topics/anger/strategies-controlling

Daniel Goleman's Emotional Intelligence in Leadership
https://www.tsw.co.uk/blog/leadership-and-management/daniel-goleman-emotional-intelligence/

Emotional Intelligence Creates Loving and Supportive ...
https://www.gottman.com/blog/emotional-intelligence-creates-loving-supportive-parenting/

Why Self-Awareness is Essential for a Healthy Parent ... https://www.ei-magazine.com/post/why-self-awareness-is-essential-for-a-healthy-parent-child-relationship

Expanding Your Emotional Vocabulary
https://conflictcenter.org/expanding-your-emotional-vocabulary/

Effects of parental empathy and emotion regulation on social ...
https://www.ncbi.nlm.nih.gov/pmc/articles/PMC7331354/

The Skill of Listening https://centerforparentingeducation.org/library-of-articles/healthy-communication/the-skill-of-listening/

Responding to Misbehavior with Empathy
https://www.responsiveclassroom.org/responding-to-misbehavior-with-empathy/

5 Tips for Cultivating Empathy - Making Caring Common
https://mcc.gse.harvard.edu/resources-for-families/5-tips-cultivating-empathy

Emotion Regulation - APA Dictionary of Psychology
https://dictionary.apa.org/emotion-regulation

Self-Regulation for Parents https://youthfirstinc.org/self-regulation-for-parents/

Modeling Emotional Self-Regulation Skills
https://edtechbooks.org/addressing_wellbeing/modeling_emotional_s

Emotion Regulation and Family Dynamics
https://relationships.auckland.ac.nz/research/emotion-regulation-family-dynamics/

Communicating with Your Child | Essentials
https://www.cdc.gov/parents/essentials/toddlersandpreschoolers/communication/index.html

How to Practice Active Listening With Your Child
https://www.thebump.com/a/active-listening

Patterns of nonverbal parental communication: A social and ...
https://journals.sagepub.com/doi/full/10.1177/0265407517719502

The 8 Keys to Resolving Family Conflict https://mediate.com/the-8-keys-to-resolving-family-conflict/

Why Healthy Boundaries Are Important For Parenting
https://www.mindbodygreen.com/articles/healthy-boundaries-in-parenting

Parental Roles: How to Set Healthy Boundaries with Your Child
https://www.empoweringparents.com/article/parental-roles-how-to-set-healthy-boundaries-with-your-child/

Your Complete Nonviolent Communication Guide
https://positivepsychology.com/non-violent-communication/

Boundaries With Kids
https://www.focusonthefamily.com/parenting/boundaries-with-kids/

Anger Management https://www.helpguide.org/articles/relationships-communication/anger-management.htm

The Impact of Stress on Family Dynamics and Communication
https://www.child-focus.org/news/the-impact-of-stress-on-family-dynamics-and-communication/

Five Totally Doable Self-Care Tips For Busy Moms - Forbes
https://www.forbes.com/sites/nomanazish/2019/03/08/five-totally-doable-self-care-tips-for-busy-moms/

Practicing Self-Care to Foster Resilience https://adamhtc.org/developing-a-better-understanding-practicing-self-care-to-foster-resilience/

Emotional support for parents eases childhood adversity
https://www.futurity.org/adversity-emotional-support-parents-2793102-2/

Support networks for parents: activity guide
https://raisingchildren.net.au/grown-ups/services-support/about-services-support/support-networks-for-parents-activity-guide

Effective Communication https://www.helpguide.org/articles/relationships-communication/effective-communication.htm

Nurturing Relationships - From Neurons to Neighborhoods
   https://www.ncbi.nlm.nih.gov/books/NBK225548/

Anger Management: Strategies for Parents and Grandparents
   https://www.stanfordchildrens.org/en/topic/default?id=anger-
   management-strategies-for-parents-and-grandparents-160-45

Parenting Goals and Expectations Must Pass the Reality Test
   https://www.healthyplace.com/parenting/parenting-skills-
   strategies/parenting-goals-and-expectations-must-pass-the-reality-
   test

Three Mindfulness Exercises for Anger
   https://mindfulnessexercises.com/three-mindfulness-exercises-
   anger/

5 Ways A Growth Mindset Can Transform Your Life
   https://sureself.eu/health-meditation/5-ways-a-growth-mindset-can-
   transform-your-life

Mentalhelp (n.d.). Recognizing Anger Signs. MentalHelp.Net. Retrieved
   March 24, 2024, from
   https://www.mentalhelp.net/anger/recognizing-
   signs/#:~:text=clenching%20your%20jaws%20or%20grinding,incre
   ased%20and%20rapid%20heart%20rate

Todd, C. (2024, January 4). What Are The 3 R's Of Anger? Mastering
   Anger. Retrieved March 24, 2024, from
   https://masteringanger.com/blog/what-are-the-3-r-of-anger/#

(2019, March 30). Anger- How It Affects People. Better Health Channel.
   Retrieved March 24, 2024, from
   https://www.betterhealth.vic.gov.au/health/healthyliving/anger-
   how-it-affects-people#health-problems-with-anger

Printed in Great Britain
by Amazon

40984651R00069